Manhattan,
When I Was
Young

Books by Mary Cantwell

·

American Girl

·

Manhattan, When I Was Young

Manhattan, When I Was Young

Mary Cantwell

Houghton Mifflin Company

BOSTON   NEW YORK 1995

For information about permission to reproduce selections from
this book, write to Permissions, Houghton Mifflin Company,
215 Park Avenue South, New York, New York 10003.

For information about this and other Houghton Mifflin
trade and reference books and multimedia products,
visit The Bookstore at Houghton Mifflin on the
World Wide Web at http://www.hmco.com/trade/.

Library of Congress Cataloging-in-Publication Data
Cantwell, Mary.
Manhattan, when I was young / Mary Cantwell.
p.   cm.
ISBN 0-395-74441-5
1. Cantwell, Mary. 2. Manhattan (New York, N.Y.) —
Social life and customs. 3. Manhattan (New York, N.Y.) —
Biography. 4. New York (N.Y.) — Social life and customs.
5. New York (N.Y.) — Biography.   I. Title.
F128.54.C36A3   1995
974.7'1 — dc20   95-13278
CIP

Printed in the United States of America

QUM 10 9 8 7 6 5 4 3 2 1

Book design by Melodie Wertelet

Endpaper photo: © Gilles Peress; used
by permission of Magnum Photos, Inc.

For Katie and Margaret,
the best part of the journey

"I think one remains the same person throughout, merely passing, as it were, in these lapses of time from one room to another, but all in the same house."

— J. M. BARRIE

Manhattan, When I Was Young

Prologue

THERE IS A HOUSE I pass every night on my way home from work. It is nineteenth-century brick, with a fire escape that spoils its facade and Con-Tac paper in imitation of stained glass pasted in the fanlight. I lost a bloodstone ring in that house, and one of my younger daughter's red-ear turtles walked off into the darkness there. So I wonder sometimes if the present tenants have ever found that ring or, under a radiator perhaps, a dried turtle shell.

There is another house, on West Eleventh Street, whose windowboxes, crumbling now, were built by my husband's friend Jerry. And a third, on Perry Street, with a granite urn in the areaway in which I used to plant petunias. Because I am the kind who cannot escape a hotel room without leaving a toothbrush behind, I am sure that all three houses still hold, still hidden, some remnants of myself.

There is a fourth house, a big apartment building on the other side of town. I turn my head whenever I pass that one, because I remember the girl who lived there and she is painful to contemplate. One Saturday, shopping at a shabby Twenty-third Street A & P, she stuck her hand in the meat bin and, awakened suddenly by the sight of her long thin fingers poised over a rolled roast, said, "How did I get here?" I'm afraid that if I look at that apartment building I'll reenter it, put her on again, and go back to sleep.

I have a remarkable memory for objects. If I were to go into any one of those four houses, I could show you where the couch was, where I kept the pots, name the color of the walls. About the people who lived in them I cannot be so precise. Myself, for instance. I think I know her, but friends tell me I am wrong, that the person I describe lives solely in my head. Well, she does. But then, so do I.

But wait. There is a fifth house, which is in fact the first house and in which I left nothing behind. To begin with, I took to it only a wardrobe of unsuitable clothes, a few records, five or so anthologies of English literature, and a copy of *The Poems of Gerard Manley Hopkins*. The last was a kind of intellectual bona fide, a reminder that I had once contemplated graduate work and that Columbia University, though not the Yale at which I had imagined myself, was not yet out of the question.

This house has had its face lifted, its bricks steamed of their soot, and its windows refitted. There's new wiring and surely there's new plumbing — when I lived there the kitchen sink doubled as a bathroom sink, and four of us shared the toilet in the hall — and I doubt that water seeps under the back door and into the ground-floor rear apartment anymore when it rains. But it did, it did. Many were the dawns when I swung my feet off the studio couch and onto a damp floor.

I can see us now, me with my wet-soled feet on one side of the room and a college classmate named Allie with her wet-soled feet on the other. Both of us are wearing pajamas with fly fronts and rope ties, because the fashion in the women's college from which we have just graduated was to dress like a boy unless you were going away for a football weekend, in which case you packed a sheath so you could look like a vamp. Allie's hair is in pincurls, mine is in kidskin rollers, and there are a few dots of Acnomel on my chin.

In a few minutes I will struggle into my Sarong girdle — so named because of its sarong-like curves and seaming — which

I don't need, because on my fattest day I weigh only 118 pounds. Then I will put on a sternly constructed cotton broadcloth bra, which I also don't need, a full-breasted nylon slip, and the pink Brooks Brothers shirt and black-and-white-checked gingham skirt that constitute my version of office garb. My shoes are black suede pumps, leftovers from my sheath days. But first I have to beat the men who share the room next door to the hall toilet and take a shower in the kitchen and toast an English muffin over our stove's very low flame and drink a cup of the coffee Allie has made in our five-and-ten percolator.

Allie is long and lean, with a deep voice and a way of dragging on a cigarette that is pure Lauren Bacall, who, come to think of it, she resembles. Allie is also the reason I take my coffee black. One morning of our junior year, while we were having breakfast in our dorm's dining room, she noticed the big glass of milk beside my plate.

"Funny," she said. "You look like the kind that drinks black coffee." The next morning I stood at the big urn, whose spigot I didn't even know how to operate, and poured myself a cup. It was the first coffee I had ever tasted. To this day I have no idea what coffee is like with cream and sugar. Even though I am now many years older and many pounds heavier, I like to think of myself as still looking like the type that takes her coffee black.

Allie has a certain mystery about her. Sometimes she drinks too much, not in the absent-minded way I'm apt to, but deliberately; and I know that on her mother's side, at least, she comes from a long line of the rich and scatty. I am always attracted to people who seem one way or another to be doomed, provided they carry their fate stylishly, and Allie reminds me of Temple Drake and Lady Brett Ashley. So she is right up my alley and I guess I am right up hers, although I don't know why. Both of us are prone to long silences, however, and we could listen to the cast recording of *Pal Joey* till the cows come home. "Take him," we sing along with Vivienne Segal, "I won't make a play for him. Take him, he's yours."

Washed, fed, and dressed, Allie and I pull on our short white cotton gloves, lock up, and travel a dimly lit corridor painted the dead amber of tobacco juice to a short flight of stairs. They lead to a shabby front hall with a big double door that opens onto a narrow street lined with tired brick houses like ours, a convent, and several small turn-of-the-century apartment houses, one of which has a Mexican restaurant in the basement. This is Waverly Place. Sixth Avenue is to our right, and Christopher Street starts a block or so to our left. We live in Greenwich Village because we had heard of it, and because the only other parts of New York City we know are the theater district, the Biltmore Hotel, and a Third Avenue beer hall called the G.A.

We're heading for the E train (the subway stop is at our corner), which will take us to Fifty-third and Fifth. There we'll wait in line for the escalator, because walking up that horrendous flight of stairs, Allie says, will give us legs like Cornell girls. Cornell girls, cursed with a hilly campus, are rumored to have bowling-pin calves. Once on the street, Allie will walk east toward Park Avenue and her secretarial job at an advertising agency. I will walk north to my secretarial job at a fashion magazine.

Behind us, our apartment — our one room plus kitchen/ bath — is dark and silent. Little light penetrates the one ground-level window, and the garden, to which we have sole access, is a wasteland of weeds and broken glass. The furniture — two studio couches, a big table, a couple of hard chairs, and a pier glass leaning against the fireplace — belongs to the landlord. We have our reading lamps from college, though, and Allie's phonograph, an ironing board and iron from S. Klein's on Union Square, some pots and pans, a small bottle of vermouth, and a fifth of Dixie Belle gin.

We have, in short, everything we need. Everything I need, anyway. There are nights when, cross-legged on my studio couch, Vivaldi's *Four Seasons* on the phonograph and stray cats scrabbling in the weeds outside the kitchen window, I can feel joy exploding in my chest. Because from this house I emerge every morning into the place my father promised would be mine one day. The place where there'd be lots of people like me.

148 Waverly Place

· 1 ·

"IT WAS A QUEER, sultry summer, the summer they electro-
cuted the Rosenbergs. . . ." That's how Sylvia Plath started *The
Bell Jar* and how I want to start this. Because that's the way I
remember my first summer in New York, too. It was hot, and
before we went to bed Allie and I would set our version of a
burglar alarm along the threshold of the door that led to the
garden so we could leave it open all night. Any intruder, we
figured, would be deterred by that fearsome lineup of juice
glasses and dented pots and pans from Woolworth's. Sometimes, soaked in sweat and sucking at the cottony air, I would
wake and look toward the black rectangle that was the yawning
doorway and wonder if we weren't being pretty stupid. But we
would smother without that little breeze from the south, and
besides, this was the Village! Afraid to take the subway, afraid
of getting lost, afraid even to ask the women in the office where
the ladies' room was (instead I used the one at Bonwit Teller), I
felt peace whenever, after one of my long, lazy strolls down
Fifth Avenue, I saw Washington Square Arch beckoning in the
distance.

There was a newsstand near our subway stop, and every
day the tabloids screamed the Rosenbergs' impending death.
The headlines terrified me, because my boyfriend was Jewish.
When my mother, back home in Rhode Island, met him for the
first time, she asked him his religion, and he told her he was an
atheist. She paused, and said in her nicest voice, "Does that
mean you're a Communist?" He said no, but I knew his aunt
and uncle had been, and the weekend we spent at their cabin

in the Catskills smearing cream cheese on toast was torture, because they reminded me of the Rosenbergs and I thought we would all be arrested and that I, too, would die in the chair.

Somewhere I've read that the Lindbergh kidnapping marked a generation of children; that, knowing about the ladder propped against the second-story window and the empty crib, they had nightmares of being whisked away. Myself, I was marked by Bruno Hauptmann's execution. The radio must have been on the day he died — all I know of the 1930s, really, is what my ears picked up as I wandered around the living room during the six o'clock news — because I remember once asking an uncle what electrocution was. "It means," he said, "that somebody sets your hair on fire."

So I believed — a belief never wholly lost (and is the reality preferable?) — that one sat in the chair, the switch was pulled, the current streamed upward from the toes and erupted in a halo of flames around one's face, and *whoosh!* out brief candle. The chair. In childhood I thought about the chair, the slow climb and the fast flambé, all the time. And now, years later, I thought of Ethel Rosenberg's peanut face, which became mine. So when I neared the newsstand, I would turn my head and fix my eyes on the dirty stone steps that led down into the West Fourth Street station and the cars with the yellow straw seats that ripped your nylons if you didn't smooth your skirt along the back of your thighs before you sat down. But what I dodged during the day I met at night, in dreams, when I waddled down a long green corridor to the chair.

Sylvia Plath was already a familiar name. I was secretary to the press editor of *Mademoiselle,* where she'd been a guest editor just a month before, and my first task was to scour the newspapers for notices of her suicide attempt. "Smith Girl Missing," they read, followed by "Smith Girl Found," and I would cut and paste the clips for my boss's scrapbook of press notices, unclear whether all this publicity was good or bad for the magazine's forthcoming College Issue. In retrospect, I suspect it was good. Just as one studies the photograph of the parachutist before the fatal jump, so in the August *Mademoiselle* one could study the Smithie before the sleeping pills and the slide under the front porch. I studied her pictures myself. "What was she like, Mr. Graham?" I asked my boss. "Like all the others," he replied. "Eager."

Many years later I saw a television documentary on the life of Sylvia Plath, but all I recall of it now is a clip of seniors, black as crows in their graduation robes, in procession along a route lined by girls in white dresses who held an endless chain of daisies. The scene reminded me of my own long march into the Connecticut College Arboretum on Class Day. Our daisy chain was a laurel chain, but everything else was the same: the June day, the pageboy hairdos, the cloud of Arpège. Trust me on that last point. I was delicious then. We were all delicious, and we all smelled of Arpège.

That Allie worked for an advertising agency and I for a fashion magazine was improbable, but no more improbable than our being employed at all. Strictly speaking, we had no skills, and skills were very important in those days. In fact, some of our classmates had gone to Katie Gibbs to get them. Still, New York was full of girls like us — graduates of women's colleges with good looks and good manners and, though not in my case, money from home — and we were all working. Wearing the store-prescribed little black dress, we sold expensive glassware at Steuben. (Often we sold it to our friends, because everyone was getting married that first year after college, and a Steuben compote or a Georg Jensen bottle opener, the one with the acorn, was our wedding present of choice.) We were researchers and news-clippers at Time-Life, whose recruiters had made it very clear when they came to our schools that reporting was not in our future. A few of us had jobs in book publishing, mostly in the textbook departments, and in some of the smaller art galleries. A lot of us were, like Allie, in advertising, and the luckiest of us were on fashion magazines. True, we were poorly paid — it was assumed by our bosses, even out loud, that we had other income — but at least we weren't locked up in a back room with the out-of-town newspapers and a rip stick.'

When I came to New York, on the same train that had taken me from Providence to New London for four years, I had $80 and the Smith-Corona portable my father had given me for my high school graduation. Allie, who had come up from her home in Maryland, had a bit more cash and a sterling silver brush, comb, and mirror given her by a great-aunt. Between us, we thought, we had enough. The funny thing is, we were right. I can't believe it now, that the city opened before us like some land of dreams, but it did.

Of course there were disappointments. We had assumed that the cute little houses in the Village would have cute little signs — APARTMENT FOR RENT — dangling beside their front doors, and that you just walked right in off the street and said to your friendly landlord, "I'll take it!" So it was a bit of a letdown when, after hours of walking, we finally had to call on a real estate agent. That the one-room apartment he showed us was the back half of a basement was also a bit of a letdown, but that we would have to share the toilet in the hall with the tenants of the front apartment was no problem whatsoever. After all, it had taken us only a day to find this place. And what was a toilet shared with two men compared to a multistalled bathroom shared with forty girls? We were used to communal living.

Finding jobs was easy, too. Allie had majored in art and thought she'd like to do "something" with it. But people who ran art departments wanted people who knew layout and paste-ups, and that kind of practical training was as foreign to our college as a course in typing would have been. I thought I'd like to do "something" with my English major, but what, besides teach, can one do with Chaucer? So instead we registered at a Seven Sisters outpost called the Alumnae Placement Agency, which sent Allie to the ad agency and me to the Metropolitan Museum and *Mademoiselle.*

The job at the Met — working on the museum bulletin, I think it was — was the one I wanted. There I would improve my mind, which the young man who was half the reason I was in New York was very anxious to have me do. "How can you read this stuff when you could be reading Virginia Woolf?" he would say when he saw me with yet another John Dickson Carr. "God! You haven't even read *Tristram Shandy.*"

The job at *Mademoiselle,* however, was the one I got.

Mademoiselle's famous College Issue was all I knew of the magazine. For four years I had wallowed in the photographs of that happy land where all the girls had shiny hair and long legs and all the boys had good jawlines. I wallowed in the text, too, about what was happening at Wellesley! At Skidmore! At Smith! I, too, was a student at one of those zippy schools, one of those girls in the Shetland sweaters and gray flannel Bermuda shorts, and this was our club bulletin. But work at *Mademoiselle?* That was no place for me, the aspiring . . . well, actually, I didn't know quite what I was aspiring to, but it had something to do with library stacks and a lonely but well-lighted carrel. My father had hoped I would be an English professor. When he died, when I was twenty, his authority was transferred to the young man who wanted me to improve my mind. Sometimes, even then, I thought of myself as the creation I know now was called Trilby. Only never having read the novel, I thought she was named Svengali.

Afraid the managing editor of *Mademoiselle* would reject me, I arrived at the interview prepared to reject her, and the entire fashion industry, first. Before she could shame me with her chic, I would shame her with my chill. I put on the pink

Brooks Brothers shirt, the black-and-white gingham skirt, and entered 575 Madison Avenue determined to be *dégagé*. Now, when I visualize myself in that lobby, waiting for the elevator under what I believed was an Arp but wasn't, I am touched by the sight of me: my feet uncertain in high heels and my gloved hands clutching one of my mother's cast-off purses. But I, though dimly aware that suede was unsuitable in summer, probably thought I looked swell.

Cyrilly Abels, Sylvia Plath's Jay Cee, was a homely woman in her forties with a low smooth voice and a box of Kleenex carefully positioned next to the chair at the left of her desk. The Kleenex was not for her but for the younger members of the staff, who tended to cry in her presence. Miss Abels would give the box a little push, a tissue would be withdrawn, and the resultant honk would proclaim to the gang in the bullpen just outside her door that once again C.A. had drawn tears. Calling her C.A., though not to her face, was how they defended themselves against her implacable certainties.

Since only she and the editor-in-chief, Betsy Talbot Black-well, were known by their initials, however, I figured "C.A." magnified rather than diminished. That is one of the reasons I never referred to her other than as Miss Abels. The second is that I needed no defense. Skilled as Miss Abels was at finding others' sore spots, she never made a serious search for mine. When, years later, a friend who had suffered dizzy spells and crying jags in C.A.'s employ asked why I was one of the few who had not, I laughed and said, "I wasn't sick enough to interest her." Half the office — the half that lived in Miss Abels's sphere — was, as everyone said then, "on the couch." Only the fashion editors were presumed immune from neurosis. They weren't thoughtful enough.

Even so, I was exactly the sort that Miss Abels liked to hire: a graduate of a women's college and obviously not a slave to fashion. She herself had gone to Radcliffe and every fall bought two simple wool crepe dresses, princess-line to show off a bosom of which she was rumored to be very proud, and an absolutely correct coordinating coat from Trigère. After a few minutes' conversation, during which I made it clear that I read a lot and she made it clear that she was a close personal friend of every writer worth knowing, she sent me to the promotion department, to meet the press editor. He, swayed by my plea not to put me through a typing test because I would die on the spot, said, "You kids!," laughed, and hired me anyway.

That afternoon I met the young man I was to marry, in Central Park. He was wearing the navy blue serge we called his Puerto Rican revolutionary suit, which he'd bought for job interviews, and carrying peanut-butter sandwiches, one for each of us. "I'm so proud of you," he said, and I, because there was no father to say that to me anymore, felt tears quickening behind my eyes.

We had met my junior year in college, in the living room of my dorm. He, just back from his junior year abroad, was lean and dark and had a copy of *Orlando* in the pocket of his beige raincoat. When, along with the girl who lived across the hall and a fraternity brother of his at Wesleyan, I wriggled into his old Plymouth, he studied my backside and said, "Guess we'll have to get you a girdle." Ten minutes into our acquaintance and he had taken over. I couldn't have been more grateful.

The action at *Mademoiselle* was up front, where the editorial offices were. The promotion department, where I worked, was down the hall. A lot of the staff up front was around my age; here I was with my elders, except for a girl named Audrey, who strangled her every word. I thought it was a speech defect. It was, I found out later, something called Locust Valley Lockjaw, which I had never heard before because the girls afflicted with it went to schools like Bennett Junior College and Finch rather than Connecticut, where the accents were mostly West Hartford and Shaker Heights. I have heard it countless times since, and have always found behind it someone who called her mother "Mummy" and grew up with good furniture.

There was a pretty woman named Joan, too, who lit her cigarettes with Stork Club matches and spoke in hard, fast sentences. And a much older woman named Jean, the promotion director's secretary and the only person in the department who could take shorthand. Only the promotion director and the editor-in-chief had real secretaries. The rest of the editors had to make do with people like me: forty words a minute, a habit of obedience, and a willingness to start at $195 a month.

Audrey never spoke to me or to anyone else in the office — she was forever on the phone, conversing through clenched teeth — and Joan spoke only to be rude. Jean's mind was on her shorthand, her filing, and her home in Queens. So when I talked, which was seldom, it was only to my two bosses: Joel, the press editor, and Hugh, the special projects editor, middle-aged men whom I would not have dreamed of calling Joel and Hugh.

All I ever did for Hugh, who was tall and thin, with the spine of a Grenadier guard and several impeccable pinstriped suits, was order theater tickets, make restaurant reservations, and type the occasional letter. The letters were personal, not professional — I think he wanted their recipients to realize he had a secretary — and in one of them he introduced himself by a completely different name, something that smacked of the Baptist Church and parents named Hazel and Dwight. Until that moment I thought only movie stars changed their names, and I had spent long hours in childhood wondering how to abbreviate mine for a possible marquee. But changing one's name, or having had it changed by one's father or grandfather, turned out to be kind of a New York thing. So, if you were a woman who had a career as opposed to a job, was having three names: Christian name, maiden name, and married name.

Mademoiselle was a monument to three-named women, although sometimes the married name was that not of the present husband but of one or two back. A lot depended on euphony.

Joel kept me busier. For him I clipped and read and typed the letters he had painstakingly written out in longhand because I feared dictation. Once, when there was an extra seat at something called a Fashion Group luncheon, to which he assured me I must go because it was the most professional fashion show I would ever see, he scurried around the office and found me a hat. None of the "ladies," as I was learning to call them, would have gone to Fashion Group without a hat, and B.T.B., true to the legend, often wore one at her desk.

The luncheon, as they all were and still are, I guess, was in a hotel ballroom. The younger fashion editors wore Seventh Avenue, the most powerful of the older editors wore whatever had debuted on the Paris runways a few weeks before, and the store buyers wore too much. Carmel Snow, who was editor-in-chief of *Harper's Bazaar*, spoke. Or maybe it was Andrew Goodman, who was, the ladies said, "a great merchant." The one had a small head, a slight sway, and a thick Irish accent; the other ended a speech on the American woman's fashion needs with a ringing "If she wants satin, give it to huh. If she wants cotton, give it to huh." They are the only speakers I remember from what turned into years of going to Fashion Group luncheons.

Joel sent me on little errands, too, but most of the time I sat at my desk, listening to the occasional ring of a phone, to Audrey's tortured vowels and Joan's café society snarls.

Life in the promotion department was strange, silent, and lonely. But at least it was safe. Up front was a foreign country. C.A. was a slicked-up version of the ladies on the Connecticut College faculty, but the rest of the country's citizens were like nothing I had ever known before.

The fiction editor, Rita Smith, was the younger sister of

Carson McCullers. A plump woman with sad brown eyes and an alcoholic past, she was forever rushing to Nyack, where "Sistuh" moaned and reigned. Afraid of elevators, Rita climbed the stairs to *Mademoiselle's* sixth-floor offices, would not travel on a subway unaccompanied, and believed that her constantly burning, and forgotten, cigarettes would one day set fire to the whole building. Every evening after five, her assistant searched their office looking for a telltale cinder. Finding none, she would send Rita home relieved. "Sistuh," I was reliably informed, had ruined Rita's life.

Leo Lerman, the entertainment editor, sat in a sort of railed-off den behind an enormous mahogany desk, taking phone calls from Marlene Dietrich and Truman Capote. A plump, bearded man, he lived in a house so assertively Victorian it defied the century, which was the point, and had a collection of friends so dazzling I am still dazzled by it. I knew about them only by hearsay, however, from the acolytes who clustered about his desk and giggled over his every word. Stiff-necked and shy, I studied him more or less from afar, wondering at a social life that was so busy he kept his invitations in a faille shoe rack — each little bag represented one day — on the back of a closet door.

C.A.'s editorial assistants, all of them tall, brainy, and badly dressed, had long, hilarious lunches at a restaurant called Barney's and spoke out of the sides of their mouths. The chief assistant's husband was planning to run for mayor of New York on the Labor Party ticket, provided he could get enough signatures on a nominating petition. When she, older than the others and deliberately plain as porridge — her looks were in themselves a political statement — showed up at my desk with the petition, I wouldn't sign. No way was I going to get the chair.

The head of the fashion department, a scant-haired fluttery woman in her forties, was said to ask her maid to iron her stockings. I'd also heard that she had had Greta Garbo and —

here the speaker's voice deepened to signal a significance lost on me — her "friend" for Sunday dinner, and that Garbo had carved. That any of these fascinating people might have anything to say to me, or I to them, was past imagining.

A week or two after my arrival, Joel sent me across the border for the first time. I was to take a press release to the fashion copy editor, a tall, rather handsome woman with eyes that rolled like a maddened stallion's. Kathy was temperamental — she had thrown a telephone book at a hairdresser named Enrico Caruso because she didn't like the way he had cut her hair, and had led a kind of peasants' revolt against management — so Joel said, "Approach her carefully."

Past the college and career department I walked, past the pretty, peppy girls who wrote about working in Washington and living in Georgetown and the pros and cons of joining a sorority. Past the fashion department, with its clothes racks and ringing phones and editors who wore necklace piled upon necklace and Italian shoes. Past the deep green room — she called it her boudoir — in which B.T.B., who was also rumored to wear ironed stockings, proofed copy with a bright red pencil (C.A. used blue) and broke out ice cubes and a bottle of vodka every day at noon. Past the bullpen where C.A.'s assistants were talking smart talk. To Kathy's office, where I paused at the open door.

She was typing, and she kept on typing until the sun went down and the lights came on all over Manhattan. Or so it seemed. Cold sweat trickled down my back and my stomach fell to my knees, but still I stood, incapable of advance or retreat. Finally she looked up. "Don't you know any better," she asked in a voice that rejected reply, "than to disturb a writer while she's working?"

I muttered something about her door being open, put the press release on her desk, and scuttled back to kindly Joel. But I had learned a lesson, which, unfortunately, I forgot by the time I traveled on to *Vogue.* To survive eight hours of producing "tangerine linen crossed with a lime-green slice of belt" or "Mrs. Randall Oakes, an enchantment of a woman with a gallant list of good works to her credit," it is necessary to call it "writing."

Still, I wanted to do what Kathy did. Or what Nancy and Rachel in the college and career department did. Or what Jane in C.A.'s bullpen did. I wanted to write something. I didn't care what, nor did I care about bylines. I just wanted to see something that had been in my mind transformed into print. I wanted to see a miracle.

· 2 ·

THE CORNER OF Fifty-seventh and Madison is still quite glamorous, what with Tiffany's down the street and Hermès and Chanel around the corner. But it seemed even more so when 575 Madison housed *Mademoiselle* and *Charm,* the building across the street housed *Harper's Bazaar,* and the Checker cabs were forever unloading magazine editors, who were sometimes ugly but always chic.

At lunchtime the editors-in-chief were dining at places like L'Aiglon, on bifteck haché and Bloody Marys. C.A. was in the Bayberry Room of the Drake Hotel with the writer of the moment, Dry Sack for an apéritif and something wholesome, like calves' liver, for the entrée. The copywriters and other literary types were eating saucisson at the French Shack, unless they were at Barney's knocking back martinis. I, with as yet no office pal, was dining alone at Henry Halper's Drugstore.

Which is not to say that I was sitting at some rundown soda fountain picking at tuna salad on white. Henry Halper's was where all the young fashion editors went for a quick bite (they were always either going to or coming from "the market") and employed a middle-aged black man just to push one's long-legged chair in to the counter. The egg salad sandwich, which was heaped with watercress, was "the best in New York."

So was the devil's food cake at Hamburg Heaven and the coconut cake at the Women's Exchange and the sundaes at the Schrafft's on Fifty-seventh Street, where one could see the famous designer Charles James sitting with his right leg crooked up under him and his hands flying about like frightened birds. The people at *Mademoiselle* and *Charm* and *Bazaar*, people around whom my ears were like morning glories or the big horn of an old Victrola, had made finding "the best in New York" their life's work. Some choices were obvious; others were not. I had thought, for instance, that if you wanted a pair of gold earrings, you should go to Tiffany's. Not at all. You went to a little place called Olga Tritt.

Out of the office I would saunter at noon — Joel was never too fussy about when I came back — and cross the street to Halper's or go around the corner to Hamburg Heaven, where one slid into a wooden chair whose right arm curved around to form a little table. The men who worked at Hamburg Heaven were black, with the classy mien of sleeping-car porters, and the customers wore gold circle pins and spoke of Junior League dances and wedding receptions at the Georgian Suite.

Then it was up to Bonnier's, to look at the Swedish glassware, or over to Bonwit's for the ladies' room, or down to Steuben for a chat with a classmate who worked there. Never once did I spend a cent except for lunch, because I had no money whatsoever, and never did I go to the art galleries, because I didn't know about them. I simply drifted, studying the pretty girls in their Anne Fogarty dresses — they had "wallpaper waists," *Mademoiselle* said, and "great flous of skirts" — and wondering if I could ever look that bright, that bouncy, that New York. The humidity stuck my hair to my head and my face turned red and sweaty and my lips moved in silent conversation with somebody who wasn't there — my father, usually, and sometimes my grandmother. Never mind. I had done what I had planned to do since I was — oh, God — twelve, I guess. I had given my small town the back of my hand.

I wish I could say that as a child I had lain in bed listening to the siren song of train whistles. But no trains had come to our town since the Hurricane of 1938 had torn up the tracks, and the old station had been a small bottling plant for as far back as I could remember. Or that I could claim to have read my parents' *New Yorker* for hours on end and dreamed of strutting down West Forty-third Street. But the only magazines that came to our house were my mother's copies of *American Home* and *Better Homes and Gardens,* and although I longed for my father to subscribe to *Life* and *The Saturday Evening Post* and thus realize my dream of a proper American dad, he persisted in reading novels (mostly Graham Greene) and poetry (mostly Yeats). My father was very Catholic and, despite a Scottish father, very Irish.

No, what pulled me to New York, apart from the young man I was to marry, was my father's promise. "Don't you change, don't you dare change," he would say when I came home from school in tears because I hadn't been elected to this or that or because somebody had called me a showoff for writing so many book reports. "Someday you'll live in a place where there are lots of people like you." My guess is he meant academe, a world that he revered and that he believed welcomed the chatty, the gaffe-prone, the people with more brains than sense. But I, bored with tests, bored with papers, and cursed with a mayfly's attention span, thought of something speedier. I thought of a world in which you "raced" to the subway, "hopped" the shuttle, "grabbed" a cab. Infatuated with its pace, I thought of New York.

Now here it was, sprawled, half-dressed, in the heat. And

here I was, opening my eyes every morning in a "studio" that had once been the kitchen of an 1840s row house and, only a few weeks after I'd gotten off the train at Grand Central, racing for the subway.

As I was racing uptown, the young man I was to marry, B., was racing downtown from the railroad flat on Ninety-sixth Street he shared with a friend named Jerry and an art historian named Sidney, with whom he was splitting the $28-a-month rent. He was going to his job in the mailroom of an advertising agency. The Puerto Rican revolutionary suit had been put aside with his first paycheck, and now he was wearing gray flannel and a black knitted tie. The tie, he said, was "sincere."

The money, everybody said, was on Mad Ave; B. had once written a short story whose hero had "come to harvest in the golden field of advertising." He had wanted to be a writer then, and most of all he had wanted to be F. Scott Fitzgerald. But now he wanted to be Maxwell Perkins. Or Edmund Wilson. Or Malcolm Cowley. He knew about every little magazine that ever was. He knew about *Broom* and *transition* and the Black Sun Press; he knew about Djuna Barnes and Kay Boyle and Robert McAlmon; and like everyone who spent his junior year abroad, he came out of Paris with a copy of *Tropic of Cancer* hidden under his train seat. He gave me *Tropic of Cancer* to read and I tried, I really tried, but he might as well have asked me to dash a communion wafer to the floor. Mrs. Grundy I was, he said, as he chipped, chipped, chipped away at my stubborn puritanism. One might have thought he'd have gone for somebody more his type. But the truth is, I was his type.

"I knew what you'd look like the minute B. told me about you," Jerry said. "He always goes for girls who could model for Pepsi-Cola ads."

Jerry was the smartest man I'd ever met, one of those people who knew everything and could do anything. We expected great things of Jerry, without being able to define exactly what form his greatness would take. He had so many choices. For now he was making a living designing textiles freelance (B. acted sometimes as his salesman), but he wrote like George Bernard Shaw and painted like Wilfredo Lam, at the same time being a monument to each and every practical skill. He could build bookcases and fix leaks and rewire lamps, and he even knew what to do when I had food poisoning: "Feed her cottage cheese to keep her digestion going and ginger ale every time she vomits."

Jerry sent us to *Les Enfants du Paradis* and *Le Diable au Corps,* and there was nothing playing at the Thalia and the Beverly, both of them revival houses, that he hadn't seen. Because of Jerry we subscribed to Cinema 16, a group that showed old and experimental films, and we spent every Sunday morning — those were the cheapest subscription days — in the Needle Trades Auditorium watching Buster Keaton in *The Navigator* and garbage can explosions and once a kind of homemade movie in which a bit part was played by a girl in my office. I was never comfortable in the Needle Trades Auditorium, because the audience was almost wholly Jewish, including B. and Jerry, and I half expected a raid. In college, B. had seemed like everybody else. Now, association with him struck me as dangerous.

I couldn't tell him, though; I couldn't tell him where my mind went when it wandered. He would say I was crazy, and because I valued his opinion more than I did my own, I would believe him. Besides, I couldn't bear to have him think me an anti-Semite. Once he had stood in the old playroom of my home in Rhode Island with tears in his eyes and asked, "What's wrong with me? Why doesn't she like me?" He was asking about my mother, to whom a Jew — apart from the textile brokers who had been my father's Providence friends — was Roy Cohn.

My mother was Catholic, so she feared the pope, and mostly Irish, so she feared the WASP. She saw my future —

barred from the Greenbrier and the Homestead, unwelcome at country clubs, and eventually cast into hell — and she wept. Of course my mother didn't like B. He was endangering my immortal soul. I, though, didn't worry much about my soul. My eye was on the chair.

If I wasn't comfortable in the Needle Trades Auditorium, neither was I comfortable in the apartment on the Lower East Side that Jerry took us to one night. There were a lot of painters there, some of whom are probably famous now, but the only person I remember by name is a woman named Sorietta who sat with her knees apart and had dirt between her toes. We drank tea from glasses while she sang "Come 'Way from My Window" in a basso so profundo I was afraid the neighbors would complain and the police would come and lead us off to jail, because everyone there was Jewish and probably selling nuclear secrets on the side. I was merely a muddled Catholic, but who would believe me?

I wasn't comfortable the night we went to a loft on Sixth Avenue for something called Folksay, either. I have never figured out what Folksay was, only that we had been taken there after an Equity Library Theatre production of a Depression-era play called *White Wings*, which it had partly sponsored. The room was set up with folding chairs, and soon after we sat down, a large black man strode along the aisle to shouts of "Here comes de Lawd." He'd played the lead in *Green Pastures*, had just been released from imprisonment on a rape charge, and was now returning to the hosannas of the faithful. I didn't care whether the charge had been trumped up, as Jerry said, or not. All I knew was that things were looking pretty pink in there.

Then another man, an actor — it may have been Will Geer — stood up with his guitar and his reedy tenor to sing some old Wobbly songs, all of them dedicated to Big Bill Heywood. For someone who'd been told by a classmate from Shaker Heights who had money, a horse, and a forehead a quarter of an inch high that her playing of the Weavers' "Kisses Sweeter than Wine" was tantamount to treason, this was terrifying.

The evening's climax was the appearance of Woody Guthrie, small, narrow, stiff, already encased in the disease that killed him. Now I brag about having seen Woody Guthrie, as one would brag about having seen Shelley plain, but then I just wanted out of that loft and into my apartment at 148 Waverly Place, with Allie in her striped pajamas and pincurls and Vivaldi on the phonograph.

In the midst of the "Here comes de Lawd"s and the Wobbly repertoire and the adulation of the rigid, silent Woody, a plump young man in pinstripes leaned toward me and whispered, "I wish to God we were at the Bon Soir."

"So do I," I whispered, and wondered if there were not still time to turn back to young men who called their dates "really great gals," and evenings in smoky rooms in which someone was singing "Down in the Depths" and "Love Walked In," where all I had to be was polite and nice and a bit of a *bon vivant*. One night when I was leaving our apartment for tea (in a glass) at a friend of Jerry's, Allie said, "I'll bet there's nobody in that crowd who even knows how to mix a martini."

Jerry had sat in on some Communist trials in Seattle, on the side of the accused, and the young man I was to marry had had a cousin who had died with the Lincoln Brigade. Together they hammered at my allegiance to the religion that had produced Francisco Franco and Joseph McCarthy, not to mention its having prevented the residents of the state of Connecticut from getting birth control information. I myself had a diaphragm, and when the doctor was fitting me with it, the ring sprang from his hands like a mouse and bounced across the room. I hated putting it in and hooking it out, and all my defenses of Catholicism were hampered by the knowledge that my legs were crossed over a gasket-sealed womb.

Not that it made any difference, really. I was not as quick and glib and bright as Jerry and B., and never sounded more ridiculous than when I was attempting to describe the doctrine of transsubstantiation or rub their noses in Duns Scotus. What I really believed I could never have said aloud, not even to myself. What I really believed was that if I said my prayers nightly, my father would be freed from purgatory and ascend into heaven.

St. Joseph's Church was just around the corner, on Sixth Avenue, and the building next door to 148 Waverly Place was a convent. Never had I lived so close to nuns and clergy and incense. But trusting in magic is not the same as having a faith, and I would not have gone to mass if not for Allie. She was contemplating conversion.

Allie's mother, whom I had met at graduation, was tall and thin, so attenuated that she seemed to sway when she walked. That she had converted to Catholicism struck me as logical: she looked like she needed a mooring mast. Allie was also tall and thin and smoked Pall Malls — "Pell Mells" we called them, not knowing we were aping the English — right down to the stub, so I assumed she also needed a mooring mast.

St. Joseph's was the kind of church that would appeal to a potential convert, especially one who, like Allie, had belonged to one of the fancier Protestant sects. The windows were the usual stained glass, but the architecture was Greek Revival, so the flamboyance of the first was cooled by the rationality of the second. The statues were few, the stations of the cross inoffensive, the sermons short, and saccharine hymns like "Mother at thy feet is knee-eee-ling" never sounded from the choir loft.

Most of the choir members belonged to a group of musicians called Pro Musica Antiqua, and the choirmaster was Pro Musica's harpsichordist, so the music was on a level I, and Allie, had never heard in a church before. Here the hymns were born in the fifteenth or sixteenth century or earlier, and listening to them was like licking an icicle: the same chill, the same purity. Their chastity made me understand why Allie wanted to convert, why Clare Boothe Luce had converted, why my father had kept a breviary by his bed. But hidden in my suitcase at home was a sin made tangible: that diaphragm. To give it up would mean giving up B., and to do that would be like losing my father again. So I never saw the inside of a confessional at St. Joseph's, never knelt at its communion rail, never again knew what it was to have one of those flat, dry wafers stick to the roof of my mouth. Instead I marveled that Allie, or anyone, would actually choose Catholicism. There'd been no choice for me — I had only been in the world a few days when I was baptized — but I think I would have picked something simpler if I had had the chance.

Nevertheless, I loved those Sunday mornings in St. Joseph's, with the hot summer slipping in over the tilted stained glass windows and the doors open on the traffic noises from Sixth Avenue. I loved walking over to Washington Square with the Sunday papers afterward and sitting on a bench to watch the old Italian men playing chess and checkers on the scored cement tables. Allie did the crossword; I closed my eyes against the elm-dappled light; pigeons scurried after bits torn from somebody's breakfast bagel. Still marooned in English muffins, we had yet to taste one.

Along about one o'clock, we would rise, push the papers into a trash can, inhale deeply of the only grass we would smell all week, and walk back to Waverly Place to struggle with Sunday dinner. While Allie made martinis out of the Dixie Belle and a drop or two of Noilly Prat, I fought with a stove whose flames were always close to dying, and together we gloried in the grownupness of it all. Once we even entertained.

On a steaming Sunday in August, B. and Jerry came for dinner. Unfamiliar with the vast terrain between egg salad sandwiches and Thanksgiving feasts, we served roast turkey with stuffing and mashed potatoes. Our motives were different, of course, but we had as frail a sense of the appropriate as Alice Adams's mother. No matter. Turkey meant gala to us, and to B. and Jerry, too. Jerry carved. Needless to say, he knew how.

The following weekend Allie's father came up from Bethesda and promised us dinner at the Plaza. Leaving 575 Madison that Friday night to walk the four blocks to the hotel, I felt for the first time like one of the pretty girls at Henry Halper's counter: on the town and on my way. But when I got to the Plaza I couldn't find the desk, and fearful of revealing my gaucherie even to a bellboy I would never see again, I slunk out past the Palm Court and subwayed home. Already I was possessed of the New York disease: a feverish desire to appear knowing, no matter how deep one's ignorance.

The next day, another scorcher, Allie's father took us to a famous fish house, Sea Fare I think it was, on Eighth Street, and I ate some clams that must have spent a few hours in the sun. At least I think it was bad clams that had me rushing out of the Thalia — Jerry had sent us to *Major Barbara* — a few hours later, my cheeks puffed over my returning lunch and B. in tow. We got into a cab, and I remember regretting that I was in no condition to enjoy the very first cab we had ever taken together before I vomited. I vomited, in fact, the length of Ninety-sixth Street, vomited again when we got to B.'s apartment, vomited long past the time there was anything left to spew. Meanwhile, as I lay heaving on the rollaway cot Jerry kept for guests, B. stood at the kitchen sink, rinsing out my gingham skirt. That he would handle that stinking skirt, that he could bear looking at a woman with sticky hair, a flushed face, and underwear as grimly practical as a mop and pail, was as great a proof of love as I could ever ask.

That night, too weak to return to Waverly Place, I lay on the rollaway cot, between the kitchen sink and the kitchen table. To my left was B., asleep on the studio couch in his tiny bedroom. To his left was Jerry, asleep in his tiny bedroom. To Jerry's left was Sidney, asleep in his tiny bedroom. My skirt was draped over the sash of the kitchen's one window, moving slightly in the hot, sooty breeze. My pink shirt, also damp, was on the back of a chair. Nobody had thought to find me a pair of pajamas, nor had I thought to ask for any. I was still wearing my underwear.

Lying there, listening to the rumble out on Ninety-sixth Street and the snores and snuffles of my three companions, I realized there was no turning back. In losing my virginity to B. during my junior year in college, in the front seat of his Plymouth, wedged against the steering wheel, I had lost my freedom. And in lying here in this railroad flat in my underwear, cheek by jowl with three young men who'd been witness to my vomiting, my dry heaves, and my diarrhea, I had passed the point of no return. There was no bathing me in the blood of the Lamb. I had crossed over.

· 3 ·

SOMETIME TOWARD the end of September the heat began to lift. Now the air was laced with a thin, cool thread and by five o'clock the light was blue. The weddings were winding down — Allie and I had gone to three in July alone — and the classmates who had spent the summer after graduation in Europe were getting apartments on the Upper East Side. Only Allie and I were in the Village, along with everybody else who didn't want to get dressed up on the weekend. Even today there is something about the Village — a certain seediness, a certain raffishness — that makes its residents feel unbuttoned, ungirdled. The Village is more than a home. It is a hangout.

When we had moved into 148 Waverly Place, Allie and I had had a few plans for the garden — a couple of chairs, maybe, and a little table. But the weeds and the cracked cement and the broken glass defeated us. Seldom did we sit outside, and the night the weather took a chilly turn and had us shivering on our studio couches was the night one of us got up and locked the back door for good.

The closing of that door marked the end of college more surely than that hot June afternoon when we sat in Palmer Auditorium drowsing through a commencement address by a former United States commissioner of education. The past three months had been a postscript to school — we were still wearing the same clothes, after all, and we still thought going to the movies on a weeknight was somehow illicit — but that part of our lives was finally, officially over. One Saturday afternoon we strolled through the College Shop at Lord & Taylor, checking out the Shetland sweaters and the Bermuda shorts and the camel's hair polo coats, sorrowful that they would never be ours again and even a little frightened. We had outgrown them, without yet having anything else to wear. Neither of us knew what we should look like now.

Some women, of course, never give up the wardrobe. I see it wherever WASPs gather, in the headbands and gold bobby pins that hold back still pageboyed hair, and in little Belgian shoes on little bony feet. But that uniform would never have done for *Mademoiselle*. Now at lunchtime I studied the clothes at Bonwit's, puzzled because I couldn't seem to find anything resembling what the fashion editors wore and ignorant of the fact that not one of them ever went retail for anything. Eventually, when the fabric department had a remnants sale, I bought a length of green tweed, took it to a tailor on West Seventy-second Street (I had found his name in the Yellow Pages), and had it made up into a stern suit which I believed announced intelligence as well as chic.

The parents of the young man I was to marry arrived from Seattle. The father looked a bit like Fiorello La Guardia and the mother looked a lot like B., and neither of them looked Jewish, which I knew would be a great relief to my mother. We sat together on a bench in Central Park while Mr. L., nearly seventy, teased me and was avuncular and Mrs. L. told me about how her son's favorite song when he was a boy had been "The Girl That I Marry," and now here I was.

One of B.'s twin sisters moved to Paris with her young sons and wrote to us about our wedding present: "I have in mind, for linens, a really good tablecloth . . . perhaps an organdy job from Madeira, or cutwork from Florence. Or would you like a pair of English blankets? Also, if you'd like a complete set of crystal, the one thing that seems to be cheaper in France, let me know and I could bring it back with me."

His other twin sister, who wanted to be in the theater but was in advertising instead, said, "Well, you've got your man, but I've got to go on looking" and gave a cocktail party. One guest recited Vachel Lindsay — "Boomlay, boomlay!" he shouted across the canapés — and my soon-to-be sister-in-law spoke of how Martha Graham had raved about her plié when she was a student at Bennington. I had a nervous moment when I heard some people talking about how you could get off the blacklist if you had the money, but mostly I marveled at how far I had traveled.

Meanwhile, B. was making the rounds of priests, seeing if there was one who would marry us without his agreeing to sit through religious instructions and sign his children's lives away, and wherever he went he was received rudely. Or so he said, and I believe it. A rich friend of my father's tried to bribe the Catholic chaplain up at Columbia into marrying us without any prenuptial fuss. Or so I heard, and I believe that, too. And I just wanted everybody to go away and leave me alone, because while I did not care about offending God, I did not want to disappoint my father. "Oh, Lulubelle," he would have said, "it's a terrible thing to lose your faith."

"But not," I would have told him, "as terrible a thing as losing you."

Allie and I didn't discuss my impending wedding. We never discussed religion, we never discussed love, and goodness knows we never discussed sex. Doing so would have implied that the speakers knew something about it, and if we did, we 199 graduates of Connecticut College Class of '53, we kept it a secret. We all knew that the Playtex panty girdle was the finest of all chastity belts, and Allie and I had known a girl who always inserted two tampons before going out on a date. By the time they were dealt with, she figured, the impulse would be gone. We had also known a girl — she lived down the hall from us — who thought she was pregnant by a boy from Yale, took pills, and then set fire to her room. The smoke, which somebody saw, saved her. But if we gossiped about the girl with the Tampaxes and the girl who tried to incinerate us all, we never gossiped about ourselves. Instead we were silent about where we slept when we went to Yale or Wesleyan or Brown for the weekend, and if we panicked when we studied our calendars, we kept it to ourselves. The night B. became a part of me — indissolubly, I believed — in the parking lot behind my dormitory, I walked on tiptoe afterward to my room. Were one of my dormmates to open her door and see the blood on my legs, she would know the truth about me. But nobody knew the truth about me or, I suspect, about anybody else.

So Allie kept silence and I kept silence, and one evening, while she buried her nose in a book and pretended deafness, I quarreled with B., who loved debate but hated emotion. Lose one's temper or burst into tears and he would say, "I never realized how sick you really are" and leave. This time I let him go, and as I did I felt a great weight rising off my back. After two years, I was finally free of hands that went where I did not want them to go and assaults on the faith of my father and people who seemed to believe in nothing at all but brains, their own in particular.

The room was quiet, and Allie, still faking deafness, was brewing tea. In another hour she would be asleep, and the only sounds would be her soft, slow breathing and the occasional yowl from whatever tomcat was strolling in the garden. This was how I wanted to live, in peace, in the light of a reading lamp, with "Glory be to God for dappled things" on my lap.

My share of the phonograph records was piled next to my couch, and I started to separate those B. had lent me from those I had bought for myself. I would give his back, the Marlene Dietrichs and the Edith Piafs, the Yves Montands and the Jean Sablons, all of them souvenirs of the Paris in which he had lived and for which I longed as ardently as I had once longed for the kind of college at which girls rolled hoops on May Day. I separated out the books, too, the Hopkins he'd given me at Christmas of my senior year and the Woolfs with which he was trying to educate me and the Tristan Corbière with which he was trying to improve my French.

If it hadn't been for him, I thought, I would not have heard Montand sing "Les Feuilles Mortes" or read *Mrs. Dalloway* or tasted Brie or drunk any wine beyond sherry. I would not have known about Shakespeare and Company or Harry and Caresse Crosby or what it was like to live up near the Pantheon and breakfast on croissants. I would never have smelled a Gauloise. Maybe I would not even have had my job at *Mademoiselle;* he had told me how to behave during the interview. I would not have anything, really, except my virginity. I would be back in the town in which I was born, bouncing from pillar to post because Papa was not there anymore to say, "When you do this . . . when you do that." Weeping, I went out into the dark hallway, up the shabby stairs to the parlor floor, to the pay phone hanging on the wall. "I'm sorry," I said when he answered. "I don't know what I'd do without you."

There is only one night that sticks out between that evening and my wedding day, the night Allie and I went to the theater on press passes and she lost me. Misplaced me, really. One could say that I misplaced her, of course, but since I am five-five to her five-nine, I continue to think of myself as the overlooked item.

She lost me in the lobby of City Center, up on West Fifty-fifth Street, after the curtain fell on Jose Ferrer in *Cyrano de Bergerac,* and since she was carrying our bus money, she left me with no way to get home. I panicked for a few seconds, hating this place where I knew nobody and nobody knew me and where there was no help on heaven or earth. Then I did what I had always done when I was a child and two or so miles lay between me and the skating pond or the hill for coasting or the meadow for hunting arrowheads. I walked.

Down Fifth Avenue, I said to myself, that's the best way. There'll be people out, looking in the store windows.

Only there weren't. Midtown Manhattan, I found out during a hike in a city so quiet I could hear my heels clicking on the sidewalk, shuts down at about eleven, maybe even ten o'clock, and the cars are so few that one can hear the swishing sound their wheels make on the pavement. Elsewhere in the city people were drinking after-dinner coffee in the restaurants I had not yet seen, hanging out in the jazz joints I had only read about. But there was no one on Fifth Avenue besides the mannequins gesturing in the windows of Saks and Lord & Taylor and Franklin Simon and B. Altman, and after I crossed Thirty-fourth Street, the only lights were from the streetlamps. The Flatiron Building, looming like a tall ship in the distance, seemed as desolate as the *Marie Celeste.*

Now it is past believing, that I walked those forty or fifty blocks without a hiss from a doorway or a whisper of footsteps behind me. The cars swished, my heels clicked, the rest was silence. No figure slouched against a building; no heap of rags was sleeping over a steam grate. Over on the Bowery drunks were lined up on the sidewalks like sardines in a tin, but Fifth Avenue was the Fifth Avenue of the Steichen photograph: as unsmudged as the moon.

When I was an adolescent, coming home from supper at a friend's, I often walked through a landscape as still as this one. In Rhode Island I had feared strange men leaping out from behind the elms and maples and oaks and privet hedges. In New York I feared strange men leaping out from behind mailboxes and the old doors that fenced construction sites. But now it seemed that there was no more to fear in this vast city than there had been to fear in my small town. I was relieved when I saw Washington Square Arch, just as I had been relieved when I had seen my grandparents' big, awkward Victorian beaming like a lighthouse, but sad, too. The only time I ever think about death is on long walks like that one, when I realize that what I am seeing does not depend on me for its existence.

I never did it again — walk like that in New York, I mean, alone for miles in the middle of the night. But I did it then, taking in the dinosaurs that were those old empty buildings as avidly as I had once taken in rustling trees and sleeping clapboard houses. I took in the smell, that curious confluence of asphalt and automobile exhaust and swill and, surprisingly, tidal flats, and most of all I took in the swollen, purplish sky, in which, in all the years I have stared at it, I have never seen more than two stars.

B. was ready to settle down; it was as simple as that. So were the boys he had gone to school with. They were all still boys,

some of them even younger than he, and they were all as eager
to embark on domesticity as he was. First you got your life in
order, that was the idea, and then you lived it. Twenty-four,
which B. was, was more than old enough to have a wife, have a
home, have a real job, and there was no reason to believe you
wouldn't keep all three until the day you died. I, however, had
never traveled, never truly been on my own. I wasn't old enough
for anything. But marrying young, a classmate used to say, was
like getting to a sale on the first day. God knows what, if anything,
would be left if you waited till you were twenty-five or -six.

Besides, I had slept with him, and the flesh, I believed,
was an unbreakable link. Furthermore, he had delivered an
ultimatum. If I did not marry him right now, he was not going
to hang around any longer.

We went to Saks Fifth Avenue together for the dress, and
he, so pleased and excited to be a groom, lingered for a while
over something in green wool, with fake leopard cuffs. Young,
and as innocent in his way as I was in mine, he had no idea of
what, besides ten yards of tulle, women got married in. Finally
we picked a cocktailish kind of thing in beige silk taffeta, with
a high neck, a low back, and a big bow. I was wearing my new
Capezios, dark red suede with black heels, when I tried it on,
and the saleslady, not knowing it was to be my wedding gown,
said, "Be sure you wear these shoes with this. They look wonderful."

"Oh God, this'll be a nine-day wonder in Bristol," my mother
said when we called her, but she came to New York anyway. My
sister, who was in her senior year at college, came with her,
along with my oldest friend and some friends of my father's
with their wives. They, all Protestants, were distressed for Papa's
sake that a judge was to perform the ceremony but determined
to do their best for my mother. So they took an enormous suite
at the Essex House and made believe they were at the Rhode
Island Country Club.

Allie, my future sister-in-law, and I made the canapés and iced the petits fours, and B. ordered the wedding cake from a Yorkville bakery. My sister-in-law also went down to the flower district on Sixth Avenue for dozens of carnations with which to frame her fake fireplace. The judge was a Supreme Court judge, the gift of a friend of B.'s father's.

Before I left the office on Friday night, Joel and Hugh each gave me a ten-dollar bill. "Buy yourself a spatula," Joel wrote on the accompanying card. "You won't be able to live without one." But I spent most of the money a few minutes later, at Best & Co., on two sheer nightgowns, the first I had ever owned. They constituted my trousseau; the green suit was my going-away suit for our one-night honeymoon at a hotel on the corner of Fifth Avenue and Eighth Street. Number 1 Fifth Avenue was the closest we could get to the old Brevoort, which was torn down before it was our turn to be Greenwich Village bohemians and only a block from Washington Square.

B. had bought a new blue suit, nicer than the Puerto Rican revolutionary suit and the gray flannel, and on the morning of the wedding got a haircut and his first manicure. Jerry, seeing him reclining in the barber's chair with his hand stretched out to the manicurist, said he looked like a gangster.

And I? I awakened in a room that I would never see again. My oldest friend was asleep on the other side — Allie had given up her studio couch for the night — and a damp chill was, as usual, seeping in under the back door. My records and books were gone, and so were most of my clothes. The mirror, which the landlord had promised to hang and never did, still leaned against the fireplace, and the light was dim and dirty. It was time to go. I had exhausted this place. Even so, it took my oldest friend to urge me out the door and into her car. "I always thought I'd be with you on your wedding day," she said as we went up Fifth Avenue, "but I never thought I'd be driving you to the ceremony."

When we got to the Essex House, my dress needed hemming, my hair needed doing, and my nails were unpolished. The wife of one of Papa's friends summoned the hotel housekeeper and handed her the dress. She called the beauty parlor on the first floor and booked me a shampoo, set, and manicure. Another wife took my mother to Bergdorf's, where Mother bought a lacy garter for my something blue. The same wife gave me a dime to put in my shoes, the red Capezios. They were my something old; the dime was my something borrowed; the dress was my something new. There was nothing for it now but to marry. My reluctant mother and her friends had, without knowing it, put me on a conveyor belt.

At the wedding reception, the maid who was opening the champagne bottles that my sister-in-law had deposited in ice in her bathtub said she had never seen so many pretty girls. They were my friends from college — triumphs, all of them, of orthodontia and orange juice and poached eggs on toast. They were pretty, I was pretty, everyone was pretty in the Class of '53. Some years later one of our crowd, or maybe she was a year ahead of us, jumped into the airshaft of the Biltmore Hotel and landed in the Palm Court. I have always thought it was the perfect Conn. College death: she just missed ending up under the Biltmore's famous clock.

How could he resist me, a brown-haired shiksa who read Gerard Manley Hopkins and knew all the college songs? How could I resist him, a dark-haired Jew who looked like Montgomery Clift and had studied in Paris and carried a copy of *Orlando* in his raincoat pocket? Resistance was out of the question. Not walking into the living room, which is what I wanted to do, was out of the question, too. Everyone — my mother in borrowed navy blue crepe, my sister in her best taffeta party dress, the groom in his new suit with polished nails and a hope he would never have again — was waiting for me. On the dot of three, with the back of my head looped by a wreath of white roses and my gloved hands clutching a matching bouquet, I walked out of my sister-in-law's bedroom.

The judge, his back to the fake fireplace, looked around at the boys from Wesleyan and the girls from Conn. College, at the three-piece suits that were my father's friends and the silk crepes that were their wives. "I can see you are all educated people," he said, and began the ceremony.

301 East Twenty-first Street

· 1 ·

B. FOUND THE APARTMENT. It was at 301 East Twenty-first Street, on the thirteenth floor of a building named the Petersfield. "Guess what?" he said when he called the office a few days before the wedding. "It's got walk-in closets!" There had been no closets in his place on Ninety-sixth Street, only a cheap wardrobe, and Allie and I had kept our clothes in our old college suitcases. Walk-in closets told us more surely than my wedding ring, for which we'd spent $18 at Cartier's, that we were now embarked on adult life.

Finding a place was not hard, even though B. started only a week or so before the wedding. Nothing seemed to be very hard then. East Twenty-first Street was a nowhere part of town, and although the el was no longer running, the elevated tracks still traveled, dark and spidery, along Third Avenue. But the rent was only $89.90 a month, including utilities. I loved the term "including utilities." I would roll it over on my tongue. It was New York talk, like "I grabbed the shuttle" and "He works at 30 Rock," and speaking it meant I was settling in.

All the apartment's windows — one in the living room, another in the bedroom — faced an airshaft, and when it snowed the flakes drifted into the warm air toward the bottom of the shaft and then rose, so that looking out a window during a blizzard was like looking into a popcorn machine.

Sound drifted upward, too, from the apartment directly below us, where a woman whose romantic life kept us sleepless fought with a long series of boyfriends. "*That's* what I think of Latex International," we heard her say one night, and we got to the window just in time to see a female hand fling an open briefcase into the airshaft and the papers spiral as they hit the updraft. Which of the women we saw leaving for work in the morning was she? we wondered. And which of the men was the homosexual who had gone to a costume party naked but for a coat of gold paint on his penis? Living in a big apartment house, with our ears forever to the wall or out the window, we knew more about our neighbors than our parents knew about the people with whom they had exchanged "Good morning"s and "Looks like we've got another nice day"s for years. But we preserved silence in the building's elevators, as did the rest of the residents of 301 East Twenty-first Street, and we could not have matched a voice to a person to save our lives.

We could not have said what we liked in the way of furniture, either, although we had spent hours in Bloomingdale's looking at the rosewood room dividers and the Paul McCobb couches and B. had bought a home improvement magazine whose pages he marked with "What we do want" and "What we don't want." So, but for a table from the Door Store flanked by four unpainted captain's chairs from Macy's, Jerry made most of it: a couch, which was merely a wooden frame on black iron legs on which was set a mattress and three pillows covered with fake nubby linen; a rosewood coffee table; and a so-called easy chair, which was not easy at all because it was only a wooden frame pillowed with two squares of Naugahyde-covered foam rubber.

Jerry's masterwork was a black boxlike structure he had designed and built to house a Ro-tiss-o-mat, our major wedding present. Once you pulled down a lid, the Ro-tiss-o-mat was revealed, and when a roaster was revolving on the spit, you could no more take your eyes off it than you could a fireplace. We treated the box like a fireplace, too. On cold nights of that first married winter — the wedding was just before Christmas — Jerry and B. and I would sit around it, staring into the dripping fat and marveling as the chicken went from white to gold.

We also had a Swedish crystal bud vase, silver-plated candlesticks, and, at the far end of the living room, a wall (again Jerry's work) that combined bookshelves, a niche for the Columbia 360, slots for the records, a plywood writing surface, and, cleverest of all, a small coffin into which one could slide the typewriter table. My only contribution to the room's décor was a pair of brown, black, and white curtains made, badly, on a rented sewing machine with fabric from B. Altman's Young Homemaker's Shop. B. contributed three lithographs he had bought in Paris, two Rouaults and a Matisse: proof positive of the junior year abroad, about which I could never hear enough. "Tell me again about the night your uncle took you to the Café de Paris," I would say. "Tell me again what snails taste like." He would smile and begin. "Well, the Café de Paris — I think it's closed now — had men dressed like Cossacks standing at the entrance, and. . . ." I would smile, too, the best audience then that he could ever hope to have.

Jerry gave us our plates, red Russel Wright rejects a friend of his was throwing out, and B. found our serving platter, the lid of a broken oval pottery casserole a friend of his was throwing out. Oh yes, there was a shag rug, deep green, over which I occasionally pushed the old Hoover B.'s sister was throwing out. The silver, a stainless steel imitation of Danish work, came from the Pottery Barn and was paid for by my mother's $50 wedding check.

If the apartment had a flaw, aside from its perpetual gloom, it was the kitchen, which was the size of a closet and painted mud brown. The refrigerator was under the stovetop and the oven on the wall. I knew nothing about cleaning ovens, and the day ours caught fire and the doorman came up with a fire extinguisher, I reddened with shame, because when he opened the oven door he saw two frozen dinners sitting inside. By that time I fancied myself quite a cook, having gone through every recipe in a book called *Quick 'n' Easy Meals for Two* that B. had given me, and I kept telling the doorman that we hardly ever had frozen dinners. He nodded and walked out, leaving me desperate for the casual chatter that had attended my childhood's every transaction. Was there no one in this city who, as my mother would have put it, "took an interest"?

My specialties were beets with caraway seeds and veal scaloppini rolled around Jones Dairy Farm sausages. We were very fond of Kraft's Seven-Minute Dinner, but I always made a salad to go with it, and never with iceberg lettuce, and I always used red onions, which I had never seen before New York. Once or twice a week we would have wine with dinner — usually a Tavel, because rosé seemed to go with everything — and it began to look as if I might really be a wife. Certainly I was a wife on the nights I stopped at the small Gristede's near the Petersfield on my way home. Emerging from the store after a bit of byplay with the butcher, I would hug the groceries to my chest and feel myself a virtual Ceres. I was going home to feed my husband, and no more was there anyone to tell me that it was time to come in or to tap on a car window and tell us to stop that stuff. A policeman did that once to us in New London, when I was still in college. "It's all right, officer," I said, sobbing. "We're going to get married."

The bedroom. Can I go into the bedroom? It held a three-quarter bed, the iron frame and the springs throwaways of my sister-in-law's and the mattress a Simmons from Macy's. There was another bed, too, very narrow, with a foam rubber mattress, the duplicate of the couch in the living room. Two unpainted bureaus, also from Macy's, one long and low, one short and high: both were stained mahogany by Jerry. Glass curtains shielded us from the men working in the cigar-band factory across the airshaft, and because we did not have a bedside table, the telephone was on the floor. The sheets and pillows, two for $25, half goosedown, came from Bloomingdale's January white sale. And the yellow blanket was a wedding present from my aunt, who inscribed the card "To keep my baby warm."

What else? Oh yes. Imagine a woman staring at the ceiling until her husband, young and aroused and in love, finally rolls off and away. She gets up, to run scalding water over her hands in the white-tiled bathroom, and returns not to the three-quarter bed but to the little one, where she can tell herself that she is in the maple twin at 232 Hope Street, Bristol, Rhode Island, and that her parents, both of them, are asleep in the next room.

We started entertaining. Jerry, of course, and a few people from our respective offices. I learned to make boeuf bourguignon, and we discovered that you could hardly go wrong with a Beaujolais. I bought linen napkins in lots of colors, but all of them colors that would go with our jute placemats, and put a Spanish earthenware pot into which I had stuck a bunch of strawflowers on the Door Store table.

Burlap was big then, so I contemplated making bedroom curtains from the brightly colored burlaps at a place in the Village called Bon Bazar. But making the living room curtains had more or less done me in, although I never ceased to be proud of them, so I contented myself with a burlap coat, and wore it to weddings. The rest of our classmates were marrying, and those that had not yet, like Allie, lived uptown with roommates and gave cocktail parties that reminded me of Wesleyan's after-the-game fraternity parties. Unskilled at keeping conversation going for two hours without a lot of help, the guests, myself included, always got drunk.

But there were other friends. No, they were not friends, not really. Rather, they were people we were trying out. There was, for instance, the young man who knew everyone, the kind who looks good leaning on a fireplace with a drink in his hand. We thought he was a possibility.

He claimed to be a protégé of Frank O'Connor's, one of the names C.A. was fondest of dropping, and took us one night to O'Connor's vacant apartment in Brooklyn Heights. Now I wonder at his, and our, gall and the way we poked around O'Connor's small bare living room. *So this,* I thought, studying the four-square furniture and the pile of paper beside the office typewriter, *is where genius resides!* B. was as thrilled as I. Neither of us had ever met a famous author, and my only sightings were of Louis MacNeice and Robert Penn Warren when they spoke at Connecticut. We would not have crossed the street for a movie star, and I had already seen quite a few on Fifth Avenue, all of whom seemed to think that keeping their eyes on the sidewalk made them invisible. But we thought good writers were gods.

One evening I came home giddy and silly from an office cocktail party and found the young man having a drink and listening to the Columbia 360 with B.

"I'll choose the next record," the young man said. "Any requests?"

"Anything but Palestrina," I said, giggling. "Palestrina makes me cry."

I don't remember anything after that, because I was drunk, though since I carry liquor well, it is hard for others to tell when I'm smashed. But my husband said the young man put on Palestrina, sat down, and waited for the tears.

I didn't cry. I couldn't even hear the record above the buzzing in my head, and remember nothing but B. finally ushering the young man out the door. He never asked him over again.

When B. told me of the way the young man watched me, like a hawk eyeing a sparrow, I was frightened. Cruelty I had associated with major events, like the Nazis gassing the Jews, or childish hurts, like the gang going to the movies without me. But adulthood, I had assumed, with World War II over and Girl

Scouts behind me, was a plateau on which one walked safely until one fell off into death.

There were other tryouts. There was the couple from my husband's office who lived in Queens and had us over for dinner. The hostess said "the girls" would do the dishes while "the men" sat and talked. Not our class.

There were the two sisters in their thirties who lived on the Upper West Side and kept a radio on the kitchen table. Not our class.

There was the young Viennese writer, the protégé of Thomas Mann, who lived weekends on Washington Place in the Village with his girlfriend and during the week with his parents in Washington Heights while he finished a novel. Our class.

My Parisian sister-in-law came to town with a Yale professor, and they took us to Luchow's. The Yale professor, already half seas over, disliked me on sight — I have always aroused hostility in heavy drinkers, maybe because, as one of them said, "You look like the goddamn Virgin Mary" — and was abusive. Angry, I rose from the table and walked home, to throw myself on the bed and cry until I was ill.

An hour later, when B. arrived, he said, "Why are you crying? You were right to get mad. You did so well up till now. I'm ashamed of you."

I was ashamed of me, too, but not for crying. I was ashamed of showing anger, of walking out. "Never let them see they've gotten to you," my father used to say. "Don't give them the satisfaction."

We went to a cocktail party where, at last, we saw celebrity up close. Everyone there was famous, except for the pretty young men, most of whom seemed to sell books at Doubleday and who turned out to be de rigueur at every party that had a legendary writer or two as its centerpiece. The verbal equivalents of boutonnieres, they dressed up the room, scented the conversation.

My husband moved easily among the tweedy men and the women in the rump-sprung skirts, among the people whose faces I had seen on dust jackets and whose names I had read in book reviews. He was charming. He belonged there. But cold sweat was chilling my back, and self-consciousness had pinioned my tongue, and I ended up doing what the shy always do at cocktail parties: I toured the host's bookcases, staring intently at row after row of titles, no one of which I actually saw.

It was better at Joel and Mil's. I still called Joel "Mr. Graham" and always would — after a while it turned into a kind of nickname — but I could manage "Mil" for Mildred. They lived in a one-room apartment on Minetta Lane, to which we would go once or twice a month for dinner and stories about the New York they had known when they were our age. Joel would talk about Sandy somebody or other at the Group Theater and John (he called him "Julie") Garfield, and he told us we could never claim to have seen a great actress because we hadn't seen Laurette Taylor in *The Glass Menagerie*. We heard about the Lower East Side, where he grew up after his parents emigrated from Russia, which he could not remember as a country, only as a place in which he had slept, swaddled, on an enormous stove. He and Mil had seen Gene Kelly in *Pal Joey* and Marilyn Miller in *As Thousands Cheer*, and listening to them was like watching a thirties movie: young men in felt fedoras, young women in cute little print dresses, brownstones outside of which milkmen left bottles at dawn, and cobblestone streets that shone like black satin when it rained.

One night while we were eating Joel's version of beef Stroganoff, a dish I was dying to add to my own repertory, B. announced that he was leaving his slot in the advertising agency's mailroom. "My God, kid," Joel said, "you don't know what it's like to be out of work."

Joel and Mil had known the Depression, which we knew only through movies and songs like "Remember My Forgotten

Man," and it had left them fearful in the way my mother was
fearful. A job, any job, was the only sure bulwark against chaos.
But our world was one in which a young man with a college
degree would never have to go without a salary. As for his wife,
her mind would have been so enriched by her college education
that no household task, however mundane, could possibly bore
her, because she could always escape into her well-stocked
head.

"Don't worry so much, Joel," B. said, already dressed in a
professional confidence that would never show a crack. "I'll
manage." And of course he did. He got a job in the textbook
department of a publishing house, not where he wanted to be
but a handhold nonetheless. He had tried — my God, how he
had tried, with his letters and his suggestions and his outlines
— and he had made it. B. was on the circuit.

My father had gone on many business trips, and now here
was my husband packing for his first: his shirts strapped to
their cardboard backs, his knitted ties laid out on the bed, and
his wife folding back the shoulders of his extra jacket so that
only the lining showed. He was Odysseus, a joyous Odysseus,
at the start of a lifetime's journey through hotels and expense
accounts ("swindle sheets," my father had called them) and
breakfast meetings. And I, who had never spent a single night
alone, was terrified.

I got through the first night, waking every hour or so to watch
the alarm clock's minute hand jerk its way around the dial, but
on the second there was a knock at the door. A middle-aged
stranger stood in the corridor, silently extending a card. Scream-
ing, I slammed the door in his face. The next day the doorman
told me he was a deaf-mute who lived in the building and did
watch and jewelry repairs at home. Knowing we were new
tenants, he had been trying to give me his business card.

If I see him again, I told myself, *I'll smile. I'll find a bracelet or something he can fix.* But of course I never saw him again. In the evening the residents of the Petersfield disappeared behind their deadbolts, and by the time I emerged to take the garbage to the service stairs, the corridor was as silent as a crypt.

You could live in New York, I had begun to realize, without ever having to open your mouth except for life's necessities. You could even be invisible, not because you were hidden by the crowd but because the crowd was blind to your being a part of it. And unless you were in a park — there were none near us except for Gramercy Park, which was private — you could not sit down. You had to keep on walking until you got home, and if your home was like mine — two rooms in which I could not seem to find a place for myself — you had to go out and start walking all over again. You had to walk and walk and walk until exhaustion set in, and once it did, home — the apartment that faced the airshaft or the basement flat that seemed as dark as a coalhole or the studio that was the size of a closet and maybe even had been — looked good. It looked even better if you could turn it into a fortress. My fortress was built with pots and pans.

I phoned my grandmother for her baked beans recipe and invited people for Saturday night suppers. Friday night I put the beans, California pea beans and yellow-eyes, into a bowl to soak, just like Ganny did, and Saturday morning I stuck them in the oven, and by evening the apartment smelled like her kitchen at 232 Hope Street. The scent loosened my tongue, set me talking.

"In Bristol," I would say, "there are four funeral homes. There's the one for the Italians — that tends to be showy. Then there's the one for the Portuguese, and Connery's, which is for the local Irish and puts on a very muted, sober production. Strictly speaking, my family should be buried by Connery's, since we're Irish, but we're also old settlers, so we're buried by

Wilbur's, the Protestant, not to mention society, mortuary, which makes us, on dying, instant Yankees.

"Then there are the churches," I'd continue, warmed by the guests' silence and the discreet little Beaujolais I was waving in my hand. "The lowest rung meets in a former dry-goods store. They're mostly fallen-off Baptists and swamp Yankees, and they've all got cotton-batting hair and blinky blue eyes.

"On the next rung is the Portuguese church, St. Elizabeth's, which is across the street from the rubber factory and is attended only by the Portuguese, who are, according to Bristol, very clean, good hard workers, and possibly mulattos.

"The Italian church, Our Lady of Mount Carmel, is on the north side of the common and is very cozy, since it's small and has a baby-blue ceiling painted with gold stars. The Italian church also has a ten o'clock mass, which is handy for the Catholics who go to St. Mary's, the Irish church, because the service is shorter than St. Mary's eleven-fifteen high and later than St. Mary's nine o'clock low.

"On the fourth rung is St. Mary's, my church, which is a fancy Gothic on the east side of the common and a block from the rubber factory. Some Protestants have been known to attend weddings and funerals at St. Mary's. We always feel honored.

"Next up is the Baptist church. It's on the west side of the common and looks like the Parthenon, but half Bristol thinks Baptists are possible snake handlers and speak in tongues, so even though it's Protestant, it's not a classy church.

"Now, the Congregational church is another thing entirely. It's super-respectable. Congregational men tend to show up only once a year, to pass the plate, and Congregational women run the best church suppers and crochet the best Christmas bazaar potholders. The Congregational church is also the one that the Italians join when they have a fight with the priest. As for St. Michael's, the Episcopal church . . . it's the same as Bailey's Beach and the Agawam Hunt. It's more than a church. It's a club."

On and on I would go, revisiting a town I would never truly leave, glad I could finally, or so it seemed, laugh at it. And as I did, I felt my bones taking on flesh and my skin taking on color. But when the guests left, I would drop into a crying jag and tell my husband about my father, about how much I wished they had known each other, about how he had had a crush on Margaret Sullavan, about how he used to say that just walking around the ground floor of Brooks Brothers could cheer him up, about how we read poetry together and cried together, about how much he had wanted to name me Maeve and about how he was overruled by my mother, which is why I was Mary. And B. would clear the table and pile the dishes in the sink and fold his lips into a long thin line and go silently to bed. Until, that is, the night he opened them and said he couldn't stand hearing about my father anymore.

I could not stop, I could not give it up. I gave him the packet of letters my father had sent me my sophomore year in college, the letters I had tied with a black grosgrain ribbon and kept with my handkerchiefs.

Papa wrote about money. There wasn't much. I was desperate to stay in school. He was desperate, too, wanting to equip me and my sister for the world and knowing he would die before he could finish the job. "I may have to will my massive brain to Harvard Medical or something, but don't worry, I'll keep you in college. . . . I'm enclosing a check to pay for your *Herald-Tribune* subscription, and please don't go broke. I won't be able to send much but I'll always be able to scrape up a buck or two. . . . Sorry to hear you didn't order a class ring. It's part of school life to have it in later years, and I'll see that the balance is paid when necessary. . . . Sorry you had to call yesterday and use that money. You could have had a hamburg sandwich or something with it. . . . Enclosed is your vacation check. I wish I could send more but I can't. You won't need to pay it back. When your tax refund comes I'll deposit it in your account which now has $82.93, $1.16 interest as of Feb. 1. Your train fare should be $10.00 or so,

hotel	$ 7.50
shows	15.–
meals	15.00
total	47.50

Then you'll have tips. Your plans make me homesick for New York. How I love that town."

His own life almost over, he held on to the future by planning mine. "I was very pleased to hear of your good marks, have always wanted to wear a Phi Beta Kappa key. . . . Any As lately? . . . Have you asked yet about graduate schools, maybe Yale? . . . I am proud of you. . . . Your success means a great deal to me."

He asked about my boyfriends. "That new one sounds nice. . . . Don't pass too many up. . . . There's no reason you can't do graduate work and marry, too. . . . I don't care who or what you and Diana marry, so long as he's a nice guy."

He busied himself with minutiae. "Have ordered your new stationery. . . . Judy's mother is knitting knee socks for you. Do you want cable stitch? . . . Is your desk lamp all right? . . . Have already bought your Christmas presents: a green sweater to go with your new skirt, and a long wool scarf."

He talked about his health, but because he had not told me yet that he was dying, I did not understand what he was telling me. "Am going into the hospital for a transfusion. Don't worry, it's just that my blood is a little thin. . . . Couldn't go to work today because I felt so tired, but don't worry. I guess I won't be as cute in my old age as I had hoped. . . . My hip ached today. Can you imagine? I think I have neuritis of the backside."

Descriptions of movies to be seen were replaced by radio programs to be heard. "Rudolf Serkin is playing the *Emperor* today. . . . T. S. Eliot is reading his poetry this afternoon." He no longer climbed stairs. "My bed has been moved downstairs to the bay window and it's nice — I can see everything going on. . . . Today the weather is bad, just a good day to listen to good music, some smart talk, and perhaps have someone read to me. . . . I love you very much. . . . I am so proud of my daughters. . . . Good night, sweet princess."

B. read all the letters, from the first, with its big, exuberant handwriting, to the last, almost illegible hen track, and came into the bedroom. He was crying, and he said, "I'm sorry. I didn't know what it was like."

· 2 ·

SOME MARRIAGES, at least in the beginning, take three people. The third provides the glue. Our glue was Jerry, who came down every Sunday to use the shower and join us in perusing the real estate section of the *New York Times.* I had assumed, because I had seen movies like *Mr. Blandings Builds His Dream House,* that after a certain age — thirty-five, say — every New Yorker who could afford to moved to the suburbs. The kind of people we had begun to know would have died first. Instead they mostly stayed put in one or another inadequate apartment and read the real estate ads over their Sunday breakfast. On the whole, I was told, it was an academic exercise. Anything good was gone by noon, snatched up by somebody who had managed to get a copy of the section before it hit the newsstands. Acquaintance with a *Times* employee, then, was highly valued.

"My God!" Jerry would say, his eyes running down the two-and-a-half-rooms column. "If only you could afford $125 a month, you could get anything." We would sit silent for a moment, each of us visualizing the same thing: an apartment in the Village with a white marble fireplace, dentil moldings, and windowboxes in which I would plant geraniums and trailing ivy. In winter the firelight would dance over the American country furniture that we did not yet own, and in summer a breeze would set the ball-fringed curtains that I would make someday to stirring, and then, finally, I would sit down. Living here, in this faceless apartment in this faceless part of town, was not living at all.

On this dreary stretch of First Avenue, across the street from a cement playground and two blocks south of a rundown A & P, our only entertainment was each other. In summer, the sun beat down on the musty secondhand bookstores on Fourth Avenue which were our sole diversion and turned them into ovens. In winter, while we waited for the Madison Avenue bus, the wind drove us to huddling together in a quadrant of a bank's revolving door. At night, with no place to stroll, B. would try to make himself comfortable in the easy chair and I, defeated by the foam rubber couch, would retreat to the bedroom. Oh, we knew we were lucky, especially in those walk-in closets, but we wanted to be cozy.

Jerry made us cozy. When he was in the apartment, with the Sunday papers scattered at his feet and some cheese he had just discovered at some shop nobody else knew about stinking on the Door Store table and his chatter rising to our low ceiling, we melded. We were young Mr. and Mrs. L. at home. Mr. L. was lighting a cigarette and Mrs. L. was lighting the gas stove and their guest, opinionated, talkative, not-yet-settled-down, older-than-they-were Jerry, was evoking their mutual amusement, their mutual adulthood.

He was also that invaluable addition to any marriage, the

man who would do what the husband was too busy to do. What I wanted to do, more than anything, was find the Ilium that presented itself whenever one drove down the West Side Highway at dusk and saw the lights going on in the skyscrapers and the sun dropping into the Hudson. What I found, however, was infinitely more interesting: all Europe, a bit of Asia, some of Africa, and three centuries dropped indiscriminately on one small island.

I do not know if Jerry liked me, and I do not even know if I liked him, and he left New York for good while I was still making up my mind. But if I remember him kindly, and I do, it is because we both believed — though neither of us would ever have said anything quite so fancy — that the best way to possess a place was to eat it. We never went uptown. It was years before I saw Morningside Heights, and I knew Harlem only as the place in which, on our one trip to New York, my father told me to push down the lock button on the car door. Downtown was our destination: that was where the food was. Piroghi, cannoli, and dim sum were a kind of sympathetic magic. In consuming them we were consuming the Little Ukraine that was lower First Avenue, Little Italy, and Chinatown.

We wandered over to the other side of town, too, to Dey Street, which was lined with plant nurseries, and to narrow, musty shops that sold spices and fresh-ground peanut butter, and to a store called Cheese of All Nations, where everyone who had immigrant grandparents or who had spent their junior year abroad went for Muenster and Camembert. Once we went to the old Washington Market. It was soon to close, and half the booths were empty, but I talk about having been there as I would talk about having been on the dock when the survivors of the *Titanic* came down the gangplank. I cannot remember much, though, only a ceiling like a cathedral's and light that was like a cathedral's, too, and hanging chickens, row on row, and eggs still stuck with straw.

Sometimes we would stumble upon an early nineteenth-century, maybe even late eighteenth-century house that the march of progress had missed. More often we would see its shadow outlined on the wall of the building it had once stood beside. It had never occurred to me till then that New York had so many strata, that the city that I was trying to know was only the top layer of an enormous archaeological dig, and that no matter how fast and far I traveled, I would never get to know it all.

Walking across the Brooklyn Bridge was like walking into an enormous spider web, and the financial district on a weekend was as bleak and barren as a desert. One dark afternoon, when a cold wind was sweeping its empty streets, we entered a saloon with white-tiled walls, a shirtsleeved man pounding on an upright piano, and a line of red-faced topers drinking boiler-makers and cracking hard-boiled eggs at a long mahogany bar. Now the saloon seems a hallucination, but I will stake my life on its reality. Somewhere in downtown New York, in 1954, was a room in which it was always 1905.

Sometimes, in Little Italy, we would glimpse old men playing bocce on a scrubby patch of grass behind a coffee shop or restaurant, and one day, in Chinatown, we ran into a funeral procession led by a small band. The music was brassy, like jazz, but sinuous and scary, too. My God, but I was far from home!

A Michelin is tempting. Two stars for Mother Seton's convent! Three for the Battery! But I could not concoct one. Half the time I did not know where we were, although I am sure Jerry did, and I was vague about the names of streets because I was always looking at the tops of buildings or peering into windows. In childhood I had tried to swallow the town in which I grew up — "Your eyes are too big for your belly," my grandmother said, and she meant more than food — and now I was trying to swallow New York. Of course I would never be able to: that was the blessing of it. There would always be another street to turn down, another roofline, another Chinese funeral.

On Sunday nights the chicken twirled on its spit and the cook, happy because she had worn herself out with walking, rubbed a clove of garlic on the wooden salad bowl. The wineglasses tottered on the lumpy placemats, and Jean Sablon or Charles Trenet sounded sonorously from the Columbia 360. The Rosenbergs were dead, and the young man was on his way up, up, up, and it did not matter that there was nothing but an airshaft to see from the windows, because night had come down and smoothed a blanket over the whole city.

One afternoon in late winter I was sitting at my typewriter when my head began to ache, on the left side, just behind and around my eye. Confused and a little dizzy, I asked Joel if I could go home. He nodded and murmured the requisite "Hope you feel better," and I left, to wait for the Second Avenue bus. By now I could scarcely see out of my left eye, and lunch was pushing its way up my throat, but it never occurred to me to take a cab. The only times B. and I had ever taken cabs were when I had food poisoning, on our wedding day, and on the day his office sent him to Brooklyn with a manuscript and he called, excited, to see if Joel would let me out long enough to share the ride.

Memory, I am told, is selective — but not mine. "Selective" implies choice, and I have none. I recall completely or I am afflicted with amnesia. There is no in-between. So believe me when I say that I can remember how gray the sky was that afternoon, and how bits of paper were scudding across Second Avenue, and how the smell of my egg salad sandwich kept exploding in my mouth. Above all, I can remember the pain. It was as if someone were hammering a spike through my eye socket.

The light in our bedroom was gray, too, and the cigar-band factory across the airshaft was clanking out its product, and, desperate to lie down, I could not stop to take the dusty-rose cotton spread off the bed. Instead I lay on top, careless for once of wrinkles, and felt my back arching, almost into a bow. Locked into that curious arch and unable to turn my head, I reached my right arm straight behind me, pulled the phone to my side, and managed to dial B.'s office.

The woman who answered said my husband was away from his desk. "Then get him, get him!" I screamed. I had just enough time to say, "Get home. My head!" before I dropped the phone and rolled off the bed to crawl into the bathroom. I vomited into the toilet, pulled myself up by a towel rack, and stumbled back to the bed, where I lay down again, back still arching, head digging into the pillow, my left eye bulging, and tears streaming down my face.

The key sounded in the lock and in came B., pale, with his raincoat flapping behind him. He had called Jerry, who knew of a doctor at Beth Israel and would meet us there. His arm around my waist, he dragged me the few blocks to the hospital and a doctor who took me into a dingy cubicle and injected something in my arm. My back released, the throbbing dulled, the film — or so it seemed to me — over my left eye slowly cleared.

"Has anything happened to upset you?" the doctor asked.

"No. Why?"

"You're having a migraine attack."

"What's the cure?" I asked drowsily.

"A psychiatrist."

Home, sinking slowly into that serene sleep that follows migraine, I could hear B. and Jerry moving about the living room and the push of the captain's chairs. But I could not hear what they were saying, because they were whispering.

I did go to a psychiatrist — as always, Jerry knew of somebody — one who had positioned his desk against a light-filled window. He could see every pore of his patients' faces. They could see little of him beyond a bulky outline, out of which came the voice of God. I would say that I hated him on sight, except that I cannot claim to have seen him.

"Last week," I said, "I had a very bad headache, and the doctor my husband took me to said it was a migraine attack and that I'd have one again. Can psychiatry cure migraine?"

He didn't answer. Instead, having been prepped by Jerry, he asked me how and when my father died.

"Four years ago," I answered. "But migraine. If I go to a psychiatrist, will that get rid of migraine?"

He asked me again about my father; I asked him again about psychiatry. In childhood I had always done what the doctor had told me to do, and now I was willing to do what this doctor told me to do. If only he would tell me.

But he would not. Over and over again he asked me about my father, until finally I did what I always did when forced to remember Papa on his bed, thin where he'd been fat and jaundiced where he'd been ruddy and with a pillow rolled and placed beneath his double chin because now he was dead. I cried.

The next day the psychiatrist called my husband, which I know only because, emptying his suit pockets for the cleaner's, I found the notes he had scribbled on scraps of paper during their talk. "Cannot accept father's death," they read, and "anxiety neurosis," and "close to complete collapse."

The first I realized, the second I had never heard of, and as for the third, I knew with a certainty that surprises me now that, inviting though the abyss might be, I would not lose my balance. I knew something else, too: that I had been betrayed.

"Does anyone have anything to say about the photograph on page eighty-seven?" B.T.B., her pearls and her diamond brooch at the neck of her Adele Simpson and her feet squeezed into and slightly overflowing her Delman pumps, is sitting at the head of the conference room table. The beauty editor, who has a nose you could slit envelopes with and a tart tongue — "The rich, they ride in chaises," she murmurs whenever she contemplates B.T.B. — is fluttering a fan. She is bored.

So are the fashion editors, but they are always bored when they're not out in the market or on the phone or at a sitting. They are, they claim, "visual," which is why they have nothing to say about any of the magazine's fiction or articles. Most of them don't even know they're there.

C.A.'s assistants and the girls from College and Careers have plenty to say, since they are verbal. If the rest of the world divides people into those who like sugar and those who like salt, magazine editors divide it into those who are visual and those who are verbal. Since *Mademoiselle* is a fashion magazine, the visuals think the verbals are dowdy. The verbals think the visuals are shallow. When the staff meets once a month, as it is doing now, to review the current issue, the visuals speak solely of the photographs and the verbals speak solely of the prose. The only people who have to look at both, besides B.T.B. and C.A., work in the art department and do not like anything they see or read. For them, perfection is a page on which there is nothing whatsoever.

B.T.B. turns to this month's fiction. *Mademoiselle* and *Harper's Bazaar* are unlikely repositories for some of the best American short stories. Everybody thinks those are in *The New Yorker*. They aren't. They're in *Mademoiselle* and *Bazaar*, somewhere between the Claire McCardells *(Mlle.)* and the Balenciagas *(Bazaar)*.

This month's story is "The Geranium," by William Goyen, and the assistant art director hates it. "Honest to God," she barks. "Save me from the sensitive."

She looks around the room for the expected laugh, and gets it. But not from me. The assistant art director sounds just like the bullies I knew in third grade, the ones who used to back the brightest boy in the class into the coatroom corner with their derisive "Think you're so smart!" I had defended him; I would defend William Goyen.

Someday I mean to track down that story, because all I can recall of it now is its title and its author. But whatever I said about it (and truly, I have no idea) caught C.A.'s ear. The next day a messenger from up front, one of the tall, brainy girls who talked out of the sides of their mouths, arrived at my desk with several manuscripts and a blue-penciled note. Would I please read these for the fiction editor, it said, and let her know what I thought of them.

The names on the cover sheets startled me. I hadn't realized that the famous had to submit stuff like everybody else, that being published once was not a ticket to being published forever. Nor had I realized how much I missed the nights when I sat up late in my dorm room with some obscure sixteenth-century poet or seventeenth-century polemicist whispering in my ear. Mostly, though, I hadn't realized how much I needed to use my head, and that if I did not, my head would use me. "Look what I've got," I said when I went home that night. "Work!"

A few years ago, weeding out a desk, I came upon copies of those careful little reports — I had been so proud of being asked to do them that I had made carbons — and was pleased by my seeming judiciousness, my seeming good sense. Still, it is sobering to think that the bench before which so many writers, some of them distinguished, had to appear was occupied by somebody who was barely out of college. "Rejected John van Druten today," I would tell B., "and passed Tennessee Williams on for a second reading." The nerve of me! The gall! Yet had I ever met John van Druten or Tennessee Williams in the flesh, I would have been speechless. If I could look at the product with a cool critical eye, I could not look at the producer without awe.

To me, *Mademoiselle's* fashion copy also constituted literature, though on a far lower plane. Kathy and her assistant, whom one of the fashion editors described as dressing like an assistant buyer, that is, strictly à la mode, favored literary conceits along the lines of "Put these flowers in water immediately!" under a photograph of a floral-print swimsuit. So I was joyous the day Kathy left her office to stroll languorously down the long corridor to the promotion department. "My assistant's leaving to get married," she said. "Do you want to try out?"

At home I spread the photostats, rejects, and merch sheets — clothes were "merch," and merch sheets listed sizes, fabrics, and brief descriptions — on the desk and, skipping supper, struggled for hours over five or so captions. Then I passed them on to B., who studied them as intently as he would *The Partisan Review.* "I don't think you need 'glossy,'" he said, and "Haven't you got a better word than 'snappy'?"

"They're a start," Kathy said.

I took home a second set of stats, rejects, and merch sheets, and once more I wrote and B. edited. "Better" was Kathy's response. "But there's a lot of competition for this job. You'll have to do another."

I could not do another. I was tired, I told B., and it was hopeless anyway.

"Jesus!" he yelled. "You're a goof-off! You'll never amount to anything, because you just won't *try.*"

I cried, and sat naked at the plywood writing surface all one hot July night, writing a third tryout. A few days later, Kathy, who always walked as if preceded by altar boys, arrived at my desk to say I had the job.

Without B.'s prodding and pushing, I was nothing. With them, I could be anything. I had lost God, lost my father, and now, thank you Lord, I had recovered both.

*   *   *

Joel and B. were thrilled for me: I was, in the old report card phrase, living up to my potential. But B. was also angry. While talking to an employment agency from which he was hiring a secretary, he had found out that *Mademoiselle* had listed the job with the agency and offered to pay $10,000 a year. I, young and "promoted from within," would make less than half that. B.'s outrage rolled right off my back. Like most of my friends from college, I thought being offered a job for which no one was going to check my typing speed a great compliment. We knew we were bright, but we did not think we were worth much.

The window of my new office faced Fifty-seventh Street, between Madison and Park, and since the magazine was only six flights up, I had a good view of the browsers and the strollers and, occasionally, the famous. One afternoon, for instance, Queen Elizabeth and Prince Philip crossed Fifty-seventh from east to west in an open car. The secretaries and assistants from C.A.'s bullpen rushed in, and when one of them, peering over my shoulder, mourned that she had nothing to throw — confetti, say — another said, "I can give you a phone book." At last I was in the land of smart talk.

Another time I saw the Duke and Duchess of Windsor, he the size of a jockey, she the width of a hatchet, marooned on a street corner. Whoever was supposed to pick them up was late, so they, helpless as beached fish, stood motionless while pedestrians perused their every inch. Looking out that window was like being at the movies, and I could not get enough of the spectacle. Being junior to Kathy, however, I had the desk by the door.

Actually, the view out the door wasn't bad either. After Dylan Thomas died, a girlfriend of his — tall, dark, and lachrymose — sat one long afternoon beside C.A.'s desk (C.A. had known him, and devoted almost an entire issue to *Under Milk Wood*) and sobbed. Carson McCullers, the fiction editor's sister, lurched in, tall, pinheaded, and on crutches. Françoise Sagan, too, after *Bonjour Tristesse,* small and wan and stared at by everyone who suddenly found a reason to be in the bullpen. Living legends called Leo Lerman. When Cary Grant gave the girl who answered the phone his name, she said, "Oh, my God!" and hung up. And everyone was kind to me because I was such a relief after Kathy, who, although keeping dibs on the desk by the window, was now working from home. Kathy had struck terror in the heart.

I even made it onto the pages of *Mademoiselle,* in a spread on short haircuts. The beauty editor had me photographed, and there I am for all time, uncharacteristically elfin and slightly bucktoothed. I am also wearing the green suit, but it was on its way out. After going to a few showings — Kathy believed that copywriters should actually see clothes once in a while — I was slowly acquiring samples out of the back room at Claire McCardell. In them I looked like the kind of woman who could dance *Appalachian Spring,* and that struck me as just about perfect: a little to the right of Village boho and way to the left of Peck & Peck and the Bermuda Shop.

The fiction editor's assistant was living in sin, and Rita blamed herself, because she had introduced the girl to her seducer. Sometimes there was sobbing in the ladies' room, and there were rumors of abortions, all of which seemed to have been performed in Hoboken. Fetuses were swimming in the sewers of New Jersey, and what was spinsterhood after all but cold and rain and a wind that blew up your skirts and chilled your legs? Thank God I was spending my lunch hours in Bloomingdale's, not knocking back martinis at Barney's, and thank God for B., who had known better than I what was best for me. I was safe, I was warm, I was married.

Still, there were those days and nights when I lay in bed in darkness, tears seeping out from under my closed eyes, and B. sat in the living room, hurt and lonely because migraine took me to a place where neither he nor anyone else could follow. Finally, shy and embarrassed but trusting because she was older than I was, I asked Kathy if she knew of a psychiatrist. Of course she did. She had visited one from every school, for disabilities ranging from broken heart to writer's block to chronic itch. "Rita's been looking pretty good lately," she said. "Let's see who she's going to these days."

Rita's psychiatrist was named Dr. Franklin. He was plump and pleasant and spoke with a middle European accent that in all the many years I knew him he could not conquer. He did not inquire about my husband, my father, or my sex life. I simply asked him, "Can you help my head?" and he said, "Yes."

And then we moved from Twenty-first Street.

224 West Eleventh Street

· 1 ·

A DAY OR SO after the Blizzard of 1888, a photographer named Cranmer C. Langill focused his camera on Eleventh Street, west of Seventh Avenue. A man in a white apron and visored cap — he probably works at the grocery in the foreground — is shoveling snow. Two men in overcoats and tall hats stand beside him, and a little girl in a coat with shiny buttons is in front of them. The snow in the gutter is piled higher than their heads, and there on the left, next to the portico of the Church of St. John the Evangelist, is 224 West Eleventh Street. Our new home.

In 1888, 224 West Eleventh Street probably housed one family. In the mid-1950s, it housed five. The minister who was our landlord — or, rather, St. John's Church was our landlord — lived with his family in the bottom duplex. A childless middle-aged couple who seldom made a sound lived in the third-floor back. A Scotswoman had the fourth-floor front; somebody we never laid eyes on had the fourth-floor back. We ourselves had the third-floor front, $120 a month and acquired, as most such apartments were acquired, by word of mouth. It had belonged to *Mademoiselle*'s office manager and her husband, who were moving to Connecticut, and she passed it on to me.

There was no proper entrance hall. Open the door and one was in the kitchen, small and painted my favorite mud brown. The refrigerator was full-size, thank God, though the freezer was tiny, and we put a hook on the wall for our first important cooking utensil, a copper-bottomed Revere Ware skillet. The sink leaked, and the only way I could ever get it fixed was to tell Father Graf, the minister, that I was afraid something terrible would happen to his ceiling. The stove was a Royal Rose.

The living room was the room we had imagined when we sat around the Door Store table, resting our elbows on the *Times* real estate section: a large square with two tall windows facing north and a white Italian marble fireplace on the east wall. All the walls but the south wall, which was forest green, were white. The white ball-fringed curtains were made by the seamstress at the Little Homemaker Shoppe in Bristol, Rhode Island, and the long quasi-mahogany bureau was now the quasi-mahogany sideboard. In it were towels and sheets, and on top were the sterling silver coffeepot, sugar bowl, and cream pitcher that my Parisian sister-in-law had finally decided on for our wedding present and that we finally had a chance to display.

The black Ro-tiss-o-mat holder was gone, along with the shag rug, the Door Store table, and the captain's chairs, but we had brought the couch and the easy chair from Twenty-first Street. There was a real couch, too, a pumpkin-colored Paul McCobb loveseat from Sloane's, and a real desk, an eighteenth-century pine slant-top from an antique shop near Bristol. A real mahogany table and four real Hitchcock chairs from the same place were between the windows. We had a few prints, by French artists, a floor-to-ceiling bookcase in the southeast corner, and a pair of tiny silver-plated candleholders from the Museum Silver Shop. We were beginning to acquire style.

The bedroom was just big enough for the three-quarter bed, a bureau (the short Macy's unpainted) at its foot, and, across a narrow aisle, a bookcase jammed with my detective stories. Two walls were painted white and two the pale blue of the Lautrec lithograph we'd hung above the bureau. There were long white ball-fringed curtains here, too, a windowseat, and a millefleur quilt. "Look," I would say, feeling racy as I said it, to friends peering in the bedroom door. "Did you ever see anything quite so virginal?"

I had wanted to come back to Greenwich Village ever since I had left Waverly Place, and since moving to West Eleventh Street, I have never lived anyplace else. I do not want to. That is not because of what the Village is but because of what I have made it, and what I have made it depends on who I am at the time. The Village is amorphous; I can shape it into any place. The rest of Manhattan is rectilinear, its grid an order, a single definition, that I dislike. But the Village is a collection of cowpaths and landfill and subterranean rivers, visible, if you know about them, because they are traced by streets paved to mask them.

If some areas have a certain architectural unity, it is not because an architect had a grand scheme but because rowhouses with common walls were put up hastily for people fleeing a yellow fever epidemic downtown. One of the streets is called Little West Twelfth, which distinguishes it from West Twelfth and is a distinction that makes no sense whatsoever, because the two streets are unconnected. Everything in the Village — the way Waverly Place takes a right turn, for instance, and West Thirteenth Street's sudden transformation into Horatio — seems haphazard, accidental. When we first moved there, the old-timers told us the Village had changed. People still tell me the Village has changed. The Village does not change, not really. The Village — the *real* Village, the one bounded by Fifth Avenue on the east and the Hudson River on the west — remains an accident.

In the years on West Eleventh, it became the Europe I had yet to see. On Saturday nights we would walk along West Fourth Street to a store that sold Scandinavian modern everything and served free glogg. I didn't like Scandinavian modern anything, and I hated glogg, but I loved the store owner's accent. It and the glogg and the Swedish candleholder that was his best seller — six metal angels that revolved around a candle when it was lighted — raised possibilities, unveiled horizons.

When we went to the Peacock to drink espresso, it was because I believed there were a million Peacock Cafés in Italy, and if I sat in this one, on West Third Street, staring at a waitress who looked like a Veronese, I was sitting in all of them. If we had a drink at the San Remo, it was because of its name and not because everybody hung out there. A lot of famous and about-to-be-famous people hung out at the San Remo. I must have seen them all, and cannot remember any of them. They were not the point. Even if they had been, I would have been too timid to strike up a conversation. Working for a fashion magazine, however distinguished its fiction, separated me, in my eyes and doubtless in theirs, from the literati.

I started walking again, alone. In Bristol I had walked all the time, long walks that would take me to solitary picnics on the low stone wall surrounding an estate a few miles from our house, or to the meadow a mile further on where the grass seemed a thin skin between myself and the Indians I imagined lying in layers beneath my feet. Walking in the Village, I would quickly exhaust the import shops and the bars, into which I peered, believing that all of America's young literary life was being lived in them, mostly by fast, fluent talkers like Jerry, and head for the docks.

There was nothing over there then — no gay bars, no young men in leather jackets and button-front Levis — but nineteenth-century warehouses, a few houses, some vacant lots, and beyond them the river. One block I liked especially. It had two trees and ten or so tired old houses, was paved with cobblestones and littered with whatever the sanitation trucks had missed, and led to the garbage pier. The street was wholly desolate and, for someone who was slowly developing a taste for the seedy and the out-of-season, a magnet.

The garbage pier was precisely that, the pier where the tugs that lugged garbage out to sea made their pickups. No one ever went that far west then, not on weekends anyway, but myself and the young Italians from the South Village who would park their cars on the dock and curry them as if they were horses. They never bothered me; I never bothered them. They would curry their cars, I would lean against a piling and watch the boats, and all of us would allow ourselves to be wrapped in silence. Silence was the cure, if only temporarily, silence and geography. But of what was I being cured? I do not know, have never known. I only know the cure. Silence, and no connections except to landscape.

Happier thoughts! I learned to cook! And what a cook I was! Rolling out pastry on the quasi-mahogany sideboard because the kitchen had no counter. *The Joy of Cooking* replaced by *Gourmets I* and *II*. *Quick 'n' Easy Meals for Two,* with its inscription "To my *wife,* in gastronomic appreciation," gathering dust.

We entertained, sometimes as many as six at one time, and B. bought a wooden spice rack, which I hung over the sink and filled with a lot of herbs I never got to use. Fenugreek was one of them. What did one do with fenugreek? I didn't know, nor did anyone else, but we all had a bottle of it, we apprentice gourmets, in our spice racks. God forbid that we should cook the food of our forebears. Instead we bought chorizo and tortillas at Casa Moneo on West Fourteenth Street, and Polish hams over on Second Avenue, and fillets of beef at a place that sold them cheap on Sixth, and by the time we got dinner on the table we felt as if we had run a marathon. Already we were giving up hard liquor, except for martinis. We were attempting wines, and dry vermouth on the rocks.

The people we had known in college had begun to harden into types. A friend of B.'s, for instance, had gone to work on Wall Street, and when he walked upstairs to our apartment, his steps were slow and measured, his suits were sober, and he was always carrying a dozen roses for his hostess. So predictable!

After a dinner party, an editor at a publishing house insisted we play "What novel speaks to you?" "Not a novel," my husband said, "F. Scott Fitzgerald's *The Crack-up*." I said, "Anything by Graham Greene"; and the book editor said, "*Fiesta*. The original title for *The Sun Also Rises*," he added when our faces blanked. So pretentious!

The wife of B.'s friend the medical student kept her diaphragm on the toilet tank, and whenever a man lifted the seat, the box was knocked to the floor, where it opened. Such a showoff!

We went out — to the theater, because that was what you did in those days, and to cocktail parties, which always ended with someone saying, "Let's all go to Monte's" or "Let's go to the Gran Ticino." So off we'd go to MacDougal Street, to eat veal scaloppini and drink Soave and order zabaglione — because we loved watching the waiter make it, right at the table! — for dessert.

We did not watch television, because nobody we knew did, and we did not own one, besides. But we fell in love with *What's My Line* and on summer Sunday nights would walk over to Gay Street to watch the show with a man, a classmate of B.'s but older, who was "in theater" and had been given a Mexican silver cigarette lighter by Tennessee Williams. The flame heated the silver to scorching, but never mind. It put us in touch with genius.

My husband's aunt and uncle from Montreal came to call and thought our apartment awfully small. The son of a viscount came to call, and he, too, found it awfully small. But what could they know of New York? My secretary (twenty-four and I had a secretary!), who was crazy, recently tossed out of Radcliffe and into Reichian therapy, came to call and brought Isaiah Berlin's stepson. He said I had delightful feet. I do.

In college, almost everyone I knew spent the summer before their senior, or maybe their junior, year abroad, and Allie had even spent a winter vacation with her parents there, embarking on KLM, I remember, all done up in her sheared beaver coat. Some were part of the Experiment in International Living and spoke soberly of sharing chores with their host families, but most just traveled around Europe, getting lost a lot, marveling at the toilets ("You should have seen the ones in Marseilles! I thought I'd die!"), and soaking their feet in bidets. When one of our English professors, lecturing us on Henry James, said, "When you're in the Uffizi, you must . . . ," he was assuming correctly. Of course we would be in the Uffizi someday. Next summer, in fact.

B. had been in the Uffizi. B. had been everywhere. B. had even cruised to Scandinavia, in a ship so notorious for its bad food that gulls knew better than to track its garbage.

He had spent his junior year at the Sorbonne, where he'd run into Jerry, whom he had known slightly in Seattle and who had been living in England. They took rooms in a place called l'Hôtel des Grands Hommes, near the Pantheon, and then they looked for Hemingway's Paris.

B. had sat in *caves* where one drank cherry brandy and applauded the entertainment — young, leftish Americans, many of them, singing "We are climbing Jacob's ladder, ladder, LADDER" — with repeated snaps of the fingers. He had eaten crêpes and used *jetons* and been accosted by young men whispering that if he was interested, he could see an *exhibition* just around the corner, two flights up. I ransacked his memory for details. "What *exactly* does crème fraîche taste like?" I would ask.

For my classmates, for B., for our friends, Europe was a rite of passage. Once you had been to Europe, you could settle down — but not before. Because if you did not go, you would be haunted all your life by not having run the bulls at Pamplona while you still had the legs to do it. You would not have the demitasse cups you could trot out after dinner, saying, "We bought these in Venice before Muffie was born." You would not be able to say to your old roommate, "Remember Pierre? That boy we met at Versailles? Remember that terrible friend of his? Philippe?"

B. and I saved money and vacation days, and at last, during our first September on West Eleventh Street, we went to Europe, with our clothes in two cheap green plaid suitcases I had bought in a luggage shop that gave discounts to magazine people and a maroon leather diary, gilt-inscribed "Trip Abroad," that my mother had given me. I was frightened of flying, but Jerry, who came to see us off at the East Side Airlines Terminal, told me to imagine that I was rolling across an empty highway, and by the time we had been two hours in the air I was a familiar of the aisle, a sightseer who crabwalked from one side of the plane to the other to peer at the Atlantic, which looked marceled, and at minute boats, which I believed to be strung across our route, ready and able to pick us up if the plane dumped.

In Paris our hotel was on a quay and our room faced the Seine, and below the tiny balcony on which I stepped on our first morning an old man was pushing the water that ran along the gutter with bunched twigs tied to a wooden handle. "It's like François Villon," I said with a gasp. "François Villon!" I loved Paris, I loved everything about Paris, and above all else I loved my husband most in Paris.

Both of us spoke French with awkward American accents, but B.'s was fluent and idiomatic, so he did all the talking for us. He knew how to order breakfast from room service —

"*Deux cafés complets, s'il vous plaît*" — and how to go where on the métro and how you ordered *une fine* rather than a cognac. I was dizzy with worship.

We walked to l'Hôtel des Grands Hommes in the rain, in our trenchcoats, my Kodak dangling from my hand, and he said, looking at the tattered building, "The day Jerry and I went to our first class, the landlady took one look at us and muttered, '*Il n'y a plus des grands hommes.*'" I smiled — I knew better — and positioned him against a wall and took a picture of him lighting a cigarette in the rain. His eyes are toward the camera, his hands cup the flame, his trenchcoat sags with water.

Sometimes, when I am with women of my age and, I suppose, my kind, we reminisce about the images that stamped us, we claim, for life. They are all French.

"Jean-Louis Barrault in *Les Enfants du Paradis*. Remember? My God, that face! They talk about Garbo's face. But not in a league with Barrault's."

"Gérard Philippe in *Le Diable au Corps*. When he leaned his head against Micheline Presle's stomach. Do you know I have never loved *anyone* like I loved Gérard Philippe?"

"That picture of Camus lighting a cigarette. *Not* bad."

I nod, smiling, at that last. I know that photograph. Only I replace Camus's head with my husband's.

We went to Ireland, too. Once, long before he knew he was ill, my father had said, "Ah, Mary Lee. I want to walk on Stephen's Green before I die." So now, I told my husband, I have to do it for him. Loving me, always treating me like a student, just beginning to treat me like a patient, B. agreed.

We walked on Stephen's Green and saw the Book of Kells and shopped for linen placemats, and one night we called on a friend of B.'s, an English professor from Berkeley who was living in a rundown Dublin hotel while he worked on a Yeats variorum*. B. had known Tom at Wesleyan, where he taught for a year or so after refusing to sign California's loyalty oath. So had another of B.'s English professors, as had one of mine, and since all three were livelier than most of our respective college's English faculty, we found them yet another reason to feel superior to the West Coast. Such a stupid place, to force its best to flee eastward!

Because Tom was older than we, and B.'s former teacher besides, we treated him with a certain deference. He lectured; we listened and sipped Irish whiskey out of tooth glasses.

Tom knew Yeats's daughter and his widow, the spirit-writer, and one day they had invited him to dinner. He asked, "May I follow an old California custom and bring the wine?" and Mrs. Yeats said, "Do you think the unicorn will mind?"

"And I thought to myself," he said, laughing and rocking on his long crane's legs, "'My God, this is *it*. I'm at the source. It was the unicorn that guided her hand, and that in turn guided Yeats!' And then I found out the Unicorn was the name of the restaurant she was taking me to!"

I looked around the room, at the faded ceiling decorations, which I liked to think were by Angelica Kauffmann but probably weren't, and at the pile of manuscripts on his desk. They were Yeats's, in small crabbed writing, and mine for the touching. I looked around at the other guests, young men mostly, in raincoats, half of whom seemed to be named Padraic. The dim room, the Irish cast: they could have shot *The Informer* in that room.

There was a lot of backtalk and backbiting and a lot of high-flying hopes tempered with cynicism, and an unspoken but audible conviction that nobody and nothing in that room would ever get off the ground. (One man, a poet and anthologist, did, and I see his name sometimes, but flying low.) That evening was one of a thousand like it, I suppose, for most of the people in that room. But not for me. For me, it was like being at the heart of Ireland — the bitter heart, my father would have said.

We had read about a spa named Lisdoonvarna and went there, to find a small town, gray and ugly and smelling of peat like most Irish towns. When we saw its shabby old hotel we laughed, and when we asked a little girl standing in the doorway if that candy store on the corner sold newspapers, she said, "By God they do!" and again we laughed. We laughed some more when we saw the swaybacked mattress and the net curtains and the chipped bureau, but I stopped laughing when my husband led me to the bed.

I did what I was supposed to do. I always did, watching while the softness in B.'s face slid into rock and then out again into near-tears.

"Why, Mary Lee?" he asked. "What's wrong with me?"

"It's not you," I said. "It's me. I can't get *out*."

There was another hotel, in the countryside, a nineteenth-century version of a medieval castle that looked like a cardboard cutout pasted against Ireland's forever clouding and un-clouding sky. Whether it was actually run by nuns or just had an order living on the grounds we never knew, but we would pass a clump of them every morning — red-faced, hearty, plopping through the mud in big rubber boots. "Chaucerian!" we would say, delighted.

Meals were taken in a dismal, drafty, high-ceilinged hall that stank of disinfectant and were served by shy young girls with soft voices and thick, wind-reddened legs. We slept in a cottage down the road that had one room, so small that the double bed nearly filled it, as crowded with holy pictures and mass cards as a chapel at Lourdes. Fornicate in a room like that? Better Castel Gandolfo.

During the day we drove over treeless hills, past pewter-colored ponds and midge-tented bogs and tumbles of limestone while I read aloud from the guidebook about what battle was here, which queen buried there. It seemed that we were driving through an enormous boneyard, that Ireland had a subterranean scaffolding made of skeletons. And because there were no houses between us and the soil, no human barriers, I felt myself sliding into that soil, slithering past the bones.

We drove to Sligo, to a graveyard on the outskirts of town. Chickens were pecking their way through the rough grass and the dried wreaths, and the stones all bore inscriptions like "Here lies" and "Sacred to the memory of." Except for one. That one stood tall at the head of a long, sunken slab and read, "Cast a cold eye / On life, on death. / Horseman, pass by." My husband photographed me standing beside Yeats's grave, wearing an odd belted coat we called my Gertrude Stein coat and a silent face. Not surprising. I am talking to my father. I am saying, "Look at me, Papa. Look where I am."

· 2 ·

ONCE B. SAID that if I had not married him, I would have spent my life alone in a room cluttered with old I. Miller boxes (shoes were my only extravagance) stuffed with dollar bills. I believed him. I think I was dependent from the beginning, but maybe I was being drained of will. Certainly I was being drained of blood. My menstrual periods had turned into hemorrhages, and coming home at night, I would have to sit and catch my breath on the second flight of stairs before going into our apartment. But if I was Mina Murray, it was because I wanted to be.

No, this discussion is too fanciful, the comparison too arty. Besides, the subject is academic now, serving only as an amusement on evenings when I cannot sleep and conduct dialogues with this woman I used to be but have never understood. All I am sure of is that by the time I went to work for *Vogue,* my

husband was to me what a piling is to a barnacle and I, danger-
ously anemic, weighed 103. "You're so *thin*," the stubby little
woman who was my boss would snap, slapping my waist with a
flat palm. She was jealous, I think.

I was at *Vogue* because one April evening while I was bent
over the begonias in the windowboxes Jerry had made us, which I
cultivated as assiduously as if they were gardens, B. came
home with some news. By now he was in the trade department
of a big publishing house and in on all the gossip. The literary
editor of *Harper's Bazaar* had told him that *Vogue* was looking
for a feature writer. Maybe I should apply for the job.

My rich great-aunt, who (like others of her ilk) dressed
mostly in bouclé suits slung with dead foxes, scoured *Vogue*
every month to see what "they" — an indefinable entity to
whom she and my mother paid constant obeisance — were
wearing. "Why don't you enter that contest, that Prix de Paris?"
she had said. Uninterested but obliging, I entered the competition, which was for college seniors and involved questions like
"What is style?" Having done the bare minimum on the assign-
ments, I was startled when I was named a runner-up. *My God,*
I thought when I received the congratulatory letter, *I might
have won this thing.*

Working for *Vogue*, like working for *Mademoiselle,* would
be like eating marshmallows all the time. Even so, writing
"Jerry Lewis, thin, dark, and crazy-nuts funny" struck me as a
big step up from writing "Plum-perfect silk taffeta, pleated to
within an inch of its life."

B. unearthed tear sheets of my only example of nonfashion
copy — eight hundred or so words about four female novelists
— and dictated the letter with which I sent them to Condé
Nast's personnel director, a former gym teacher with the manner, and command, of a mother superior. A few weeks later I
found myself sitting in *Vogue's* enormous waiting room, which
was furnished with the kind of spindly chairs and tables I knew

from Miss Dutton's Tearoom in Providence, Rhode Island, and painted eau de Nile and silver. "Found myself" because, strictly speaking, I had not really arrived there under my own steam.

Would that I had had a sense of the ridiculous! Would that I had not been as sober as an owl, as judgmental as Cotton Mather! I might have dined out on life in *Vogue*'s feature department. Instead I stayed in to cry.

What a cast! Were the women who worked on fashion magazines like *Vogue* in the late fifties crazier than the ones who work on them today? (*Mademoiselle*, but for its fashion editors, attracted more bookish types, the kind who later staffed publishing houses.) Or is it that I, small-town and shy, saw anyone whose sophistication exceeded mine as exotic? I have given the matter much thought, another of my dialogues for sleepless nights, and have decided on the former. The late fifties at *Vogue*, and presumably *Bazaar*, represented the madwoman's last hurrah.

My researcher — the title given to secretaries at the magazine so they would not realize they were secretaries — was small, pretty, eager, and married to a homosexual. She had met him in Paris during her (and his) junior year abroad, and with its being Paris and her having read a lot and him wanting to write a lot, she confused him with André Gide and was wed.

They lived on the Upper West Side, next door to the fiction editor of *Esquire*, into whose apartment they could peer from their bedroom window. The fiction editor, who didn't know of their presence and indeed never met them, worked nights at his kitchen table under their constant surveillance. Aided by binoculars, they would try to spot the moment when his eyes fell on one of the husband's manuscripts and thereby study his facial reactions.

Their night watches struck me as peculiar, as did her happy smile when she told me she was leaving him of whom she spoke so lovingly, so I wasn't surprised when her parents swept into New York and had her committed to a sanatorium. She was a not atypical employee.

I should add that on the second day I worked at *Vogue,* I was told never to use her as a researcher, since she was unreliable. Since good typing was beyond her as well, I soon decided that her real role, apart from bringing in the tea and cookies that arrived on our desks every day at four, was to be one of the cloud of butterflies hired by the personnel department to decorate the place and disguise the fact that the rest of the employees were worker bees or praying mantises.

The second researcher was a butterfly, too, a tall dim girl from Bernardsville, New Jersey, who spent every weekend in Maine with her fiancé's family, flown there by the family plane. Once, grumbling slightly about having lost a brooch at a wedding reception, she brought me the insurance form so I could check her spelling and I saw that the pin was valued at $3,000, or more than half her salary. Again, a not atypical employee.

She had literary ambitions and wrote occasional captions, which, like all our captions, were thick with adjectives and strong verbs and adhered to the rule of three: each subject got three modifiers. A movie actress might be "beautiful, brainy, and unexpectedly bizarre"; a movie actor, "russet-haired, impish, and crinkle-grinned." Eighteenth-century artists were often called upon. All fair-haired women looked like Greuzes to us; and Brigitte Bardot was compared to Boucher's Mademoiselle O'Murphy. A small woman was invariably a Tanagra figurine, and when in doubt we relied on "extraordinary."

The woman with whom I shared an office — a perfect cube with two old desks, a cracked ceiling, peeling paint, and a travel poster depending from one strip of Scotch tape — was a rarity, a combination butterfly and worker bee. Her hair bubbled blond and her eyes flashed blue and she spoke with an international accent, crisp and faintly British.

Her former husband, the author of "the definitive book on

the Argentine pampas," she said, had run through all her money, and she was living in a small apartment on Park Avenue. She slept there, dressed there, received her dinner dates there, but never saw the inside of the kitchen unless she was pouring herself a morning glass of orange juice. No embassy gave a dinner party without her, since she spoke four or five languages and could be depended upon to beguile all visiting foreigners. She had been the girlfriend of a famous movie star and a close friend of a famous conductor and, desperate to remarry, would one day land a French diplomat — "It was a *coup de foudre*, Mary, an absolute *coup de foudre*" — whose previous marriages she dismissed by saying, "The first was when he was very young, so we'll overlook *that*, and the second was to a Pole, which doesn't count because nobody can stay married to a Pole."

Under the bubbles, however, was a hard head and, I found, surprised because she prattled of her Virginia birth in such a way as to make one think she was every Byrd, Lee, and Carter rolled into one, a lapsed Catholicism of the Irish variety. Whenever one or the other of us was called to the mat by our editor, we exchanged signs of the cross and laugh-punctuated Hail Marys.

Down the hall worked Margaret Case, the society editor, though she was never known by so definitive and essentially déclassé a title. A friend to the rich, a brute to her researchers, she was not unkind to me. When I had to write about Newport, she hovered over the phone while I called the wife of the man who had revived the old Newport Casino to ask about the exact color of the new shingles, and, satisfied that I had not shamed *Vogue* with my gaucherie, proceeded to put a little trust (not much) in my intelligence. When she finished the draft of a letter to the princesse de Rethy, the king of Belgium's consort, for instance, she brought it to me for editing, although I was, still am, the last person to ask about protocol and royalty. When she had to make phone calls about a sad, poor sister, I think it was, she made them from my office, trusting that I would not talk.

When I wrote of somebody's "magnificent Venetian palazzo," she told me to strike "magnificent." "I've seen better," she growled. And when (or so I was told) she talked the archbishop of Canterbury into being photographed by Penn or somebody like Penn, she ended the telephone conversation with a peremptory "And wear your robes!" One month she went to Greece, and I, excited at the prospect of anyone's going to Greece, asked her if she had been there before. "Only on the Onassis yacht," she said.

Miss Case had no jewelry, no jewelry that counted anyway, and whenever I went into her office she was phoning someone called "Darling Vava" and telling him that Mrs. Luce said she could borrow her sapphires for that evening and would he please get them out and she'd send her researcher for them. There was something noble about her, I thought, struggling into a girdle and an evening gown night after night and smearing orange lipstick across her thin, impatient mouth.

A long time later, after she had forgotten my name and where she had known me, we shared an elevator. She remembered my face and said, "Tell me. I just got a letter from a friend's daughter who wants to work for a magazine. Tell me. Was typing a great help to you in your career?" "Yes, it was," I said, and we never spoke again, although I often saw her hailing cabs. When she killed herself, jumping fourteen stories naked under the plaid raincoat that was her all-weather uniform, I was truly sorry, because she had been nice to me, knowing that I knew she was an outsider, never mind the rich friends, and liked her anyway.

Now we come to my editor, Allene Talmey, Allene who was as short and firmly packed as a Boston bull and had a Boston bull's bright brown eyes. She never showed up before eleven in the morning and never left before seven at night, and she worked out of a small, plain office with a Tamayo of a water-melon on one wall. Her desk and desk chair were mounted on a thick pad, presumably to save the rug. But the pad also served to raise her above whomever she was talking to, which always struck me as the point.

On my first day at *Vogue,* she dumped on my desk a pile of research, all of it in French, which was to help me in my first assignment: deep captions, as we called them, for some Penn photographs of elderly French notables. No one, certainly not she, had ever asked me if I read French. It was an assumption, as taken for granted there as one's washing one's hands before leaving the ladies' room. It was also, less innocently, a way of separating the sheep from the goats.

I do read French, so I passed the test. The test I could not pass was lining up the requisite modifiers, at least one of which had to be unexpected, tap-dancing through the middle and coming up with a smash finish. When I would go to Allene for help, she would tell me that what I had done was wrong, all wrong, but she would never say or show me why. I would study the caption and, not having been given an exit from my sentences and unable to find one on my own, would grow as dizzy and frantic as a rat in a maze.

Where to go for research was another problem. One of the notables was a sculptor of whom I had never heard. When I asked Allene where I could get more information, she told me to go to the owner of the gallery that showed his work. But when the same problem arose with another artist (the notables were certainly that, but they were also obscure) and I suggested going to his dealer, her reply was "Don't you know that's the worst gallery in New York?" She said nothing further, so I returned to my desk, stared at the material, didn't know who else to call, and felt the start of the paralysis that eventually swallowed me.

I would go out to interview the famous, become so involved with talking to them that I forgot their fame and my fear, and return with good, often funny notes. But once I was back in the Graybar Building, where *Vogue* had its offices, and aware that Allene's sharp tongue was about to rip my back, I was terrified. One day she outdid herself — outdid everyone, really, who has ever disliked me. "You have more talent for the quick phrase than anyone I've ever hired," she barked, "but you're not capable of a sustained piece of work."

Using my notes — "After Loren, bones are boring" was perhaps my finest moment — Allene would write the captions, bring them out to be typed, and then, always running scared, wait for our reactions to them. Since they were good within their context and entirely predictable, I had nothing to say, having been raised never to gush or, in my family's parlance, be "Judas-friendly." My silence meant acceptance, but it was construed as criticism, and I was stunned the day she asked, "Do you know how many people you've hurt?"

When I joked of the horror of having to write my fifth caption in one day about women about whom there was little to say except that they had "skin as translucent as a Limoges cup" and "a brave list of charities," she heard of it within seconds and raged at what she called my betrayal. Her secretary and her assistant, linked in the camaraderie of survivorship, let me flounder. Only my friend the bubbly blonde implied that Allene was difficult to work for. "The first few weeks I worked with her . . . well, my dear, I used to go home, sit in the tub, and *weep.* My dear, the bathwater was pure salt." I wish I had known about the walking wounded who were my predecessors, or that one of them had spoken of wanting to kill Allene and claimed she lay in bed at night trying to figure out how to leave the Graybar undetected. It might have given me a new perspective.

By then, however, I had no perspective on anything, and certainly not *Vogue.* I had even begun to believe in "People Are

Talking About." This was a page, written primarily by Allene from material collected by her minions, that ran in almost every issue. Finding "People" items was a nightmare. If we were lucky, we could come up with sentences like "People Are Talking About . . . the bluesy, cigarette-rasp with which the astonishing Elaine Stritch saws through 'You Took Advantage of Me'. . . the way the brilliant young senator from Massachusetts, John F. Kennedy, is capturing the nation's imagination." Unlucky, we were reduced, as one contributor once was, to ". . . the music piped into the treatment rooms at Sloan-Kettering during chemotherapy."

I wrote a "People" page all by myself once, when Allene was on holiday — "on holiday," so snugly British, was *Vogue*'s preferred term for two weeks with pay — and Jessica Daves, the magazine's faintly frumpy editor-in-chief, suddenly wanted one. With the bull terrier no longer a room away, my pencil flew. Once she was back, it traced boxes and initials and trees with fluffy tops, but no sentences. Allene threatened to fire me, but I said no, you must not, because I have never failed at anything and cannot bear to.

One autumn afternoon I walked to Saks Fifth Avenue to buy a dress I had seen in an advertisement. I had never cared much about clothes, except for the samples I bought from McCardell's back room, and was vain only of my very narrow feet. The one mirror in our apartment was on the door of the medicine cabinet. Mornings, I would sling on something, twist my head over my shoulder to see if my slip showed, and that was it. So I did not know what I looked like until I saw myself in the dressing room's full-length mirror: ghastly in orange, my cheeks as hollow as if I had lost my back teeth, my eyes as staring as my father's just before he died, my arms like sticks.

Only Jell-O would go down at lunch, Jell-O and the occasional nutted cream cheese sandwich at the Chock Full O' Nuts across Lexington from the Graybar, and the Dexamyl that

Dr. Franklin had prescribed was robbing me of what little appetite was left. B. joked about my logorrhea, about how I would elbow him awake at midnight with "Did I ever tell you what my grandfather said to me when I was ten?" and "Do you remember the time we went to the basketball game and . . . ?" but he could not joke any more after he took me, for a treat, to a restaurant named Teddy's.

Teddy's was a treat because it was expensive and because we had convinced ourselves the other customers were Mafia. It was a treat, too, because it was somewhere around the west end of Canal Street, and the kind of New Yorkers we were turning into love nothing more than eating in a nowhere part of town. The walls above the banquettes were lined with photographs of Teddy's movie-star diners, and we sat directly under one of Elizabeth Taylor, who was at that moment supposed to be dying. It should have been a wonderful evening, what with the rain falling sadly on Canal Street and the beautiful young actress so tragically breathing her last and B., who looked so much like Montgomery Clift in *A Place in the Sun,* sitting beside me. But when the steamed lobster I'd ordered arrived, out of its shell and lying naked on a bed of lettuce, I thought it looked like a boiled baby. Perhaps it was the Dexamyl; perhaps it was Allene. All I know is that when I saw that lobster nestled in its iceberg lettuce cradle, I saw a murdered child.

I lasted for about nine months, or maybe it was seven, until the winter morning when I wrote a deep caption about an actress. It was a monument to adjectives, strong verbs, and the rule of three, and Allene liked it. She even smiled. Still, there was something wrong — she didn't say what — with the last sentence. I slid the paper off her desk, stood up, and did what I should have done a long time before. I said, "I quit."

"You can't do that," Allene barked, then, terrier to the last, added, "I don't care if you spend the rest of the week in the infirmary, but no one just walks out of here."

"I do," I replied, and left her office.

Pausing only to pick up the stone from Prince Edward Island that I was using as a paperweight and the cellophane bag of dried apricots with which I was trying to beef up my blood, I ran for the elevator and home. There I did what I always did when I had lost my temper. I cried.

B. took me to the Berkshires the following weekend, to an inn that served up roast ham and raisin sauce and four-poster beds and cranberry-glass tumblers. We had longed to go to an inn like that, and to auctions, where we could at last buy the hutch and dry sink that would make us feel calm and cozy and truly married. But by now I was seeing the world through the wrong end of a telescope. Everything and everyone was very far away, too far away to touch or be touched by. One afternoon, so late that shadows were already bluing the snow, I took a long solitary walk beside the river. Walking, the mere act of moving my legs, had always brought me back into connection with the physical. But this time I returned shaking, because I believed that someone, shielded by the tall snowbanks that margined the water, was tracking my every step.

A few months later, a woman, a stranger, called me at home. My replacement at *Vogue*, she had found my name in the files and was wondering if I could tell her something about her boss, because no one else would talk. I didn't talk either. I thought the phone was bugged.

Years later, I ran into Allene at a cocktail party. She congratulated me on what I was doing and I congratulated her on what she was doing, half expecting the playful slap and the sputtered "You're so *thin!*" Then we both disappeared into the smoke and the chatter and the palazzo pajamas and the dry vermouth on the rocks, and I never saw her again. I never forgave her, either, not for being demanding but for being unable to resist piercing an all-too-visible jugular vein.

* * *

A man and a woman are sitting at night in a living room in Greenwich Village. It is nicely furnished and so are they. Both are reading. The woman is lonely, she is always lonely, and she would like to ask her husband if she could sit in his lap. He would like that. But if she does, she will feel his penis rise and push against her buttocks, and that will shock and sicken her. When he stands up she would like to go to him. But if she does, he will press his groin against hers and his penis will swell and she will loosen her arms and push him away. She would like to look at him. But if she does, he will mistake the glance and cross the room to her. Therefore she does not dare to ask to sit in his lap or hug him or even look at him. So she is silent and motionless and he is silent and motionless, and the one keeps her head bent over Ngaio Marsh and the other keeps his head bent over Philip Rahv.

It is a few days before Christmas. The woman has put up a tree and the man has helped decorate it and both are especially pleased with a jeweled butterfly she bought on Madison Avenue. Christmas cards march across the quasi-mahogany sideboard and wrapping paper spills from the couch. She has made cookies and he has made elaborate efforts to hide his presents to her in their apartment's one closet. She was excited about Christmas coming and December's briskness and her forays along Fifth Avenue, because he is beginning to make enough money for them to spend a bit. But now she has stopped talking and cannot hear when he speaks, because today she saw a man holding a little girl's hand while together they looked in a window of FAO Schwarz and suddenly she wanted to be dead.

An evening a day or two later. The man and woman are walking home from dinner at a friend's house. There was a girl there, younger than she and even shyer, and because the woman felt sorry for her she "brought her out," as her mother would have put it, and made her comfortable. The man is proud of his wife. "You couldn't have done that a few years ago," he says, and the woman grins. She has just received an A+.

Any Tuesday or Thursday at 4:30 in a psychiatrist's office in Schwab House, on the Upper West Side, which is where all psychiatrists seemed to have their offices. Given the Jewish and Austrian accents that overlay the area like icing on a cake, the woman assumes the placement brings Freud's acolytes closer to him.

The woman is sitting, arms and legs crossed, on a Barcelona chair. The couch to her left, also from Mies, has a clean paper towel, changed for each patient, at its head. But not for her. She has never lain on the couch and she never will.

The doctor is smiling, because the woman can be rather amusing, but although she talks a lot, she says nothing. After their fifty-minute session, she walks to the Seventy-second Street stop of the IRT and descends the narrow stairs to the track. When she hears the train coming, she steps behind a pillar and closes her eyes. She is afraid that if she sees it, she will jump.

The woman loves her husband. No, incorrect. She worships her husband. But she wants to go to her father. Suicide, however, is out of the question. She is a coward, and besides, her church, whose grasp she has never quite managed to elude, will not let her. So what is she to do? Writing is out of the question: she believes what she was told, that she is "not capable of a sustained piece of work." Another job is out of the question: she has already worked for two magazines and where else can she go? A baby is out of the question: her gynecologist says she is too underweight to risk pregnancy. There is nothing for it but to move.

21 Perry Street

· 1 ·

SOMEWHERE I have read that an image John Fowles could not get out of his head, of a hooded figure alone on a dock, was what prompted him to write *The French Lieutenant's Woman.* There is an image I cannot get out of my head, either, that of a man standing in the areaway of our third apartment, and although it has never prompted me to write a novel, it has always struck me as a compelling first page.

The page, in précis, would read something like this. A young man and a young woman are walking home from the late show at the Waverly Theater in Greenwich Village, where they live. It is a hot summer night, and their steps are as slow as their conversation is lazy. As they round the corner of Perry Street, they see, silhouetted against the white petunias the young woman has planted in an old concrete urn, a man standing in the areaway of their apartment. He is motionless. Perhaps he is listening to something. Or waiting.

In reality, the young man and woman keep on walking, passing their apartment as if it were not theirs at all. When they return, ten or so minutes later, from their circuit of the block, the man is gone. The hands that gripped their hearts relax. They can enter the areaway, unlock the second gate, go home.

On my first page, however, the young couple decide to dare the intruder in the areaway. Maybe it is just that he is at the wrong address. The night is dark, and all these houses, brick with tall stoops, look alike. So they open the first gate, the latched one that abuts the sidewalk, and ask the man if they can help him. He mutters something, then moves toward the gate they have just opened. Relieved, they turn to the second gate, and the young man brings out his keys. Then it happens. The stranger swivels and plunges a knife in the young man's back. The woman, her shoulders hunched and her own back pressed against the areaway's brownstone facing, watches her husband die. Meanwhile the stranger, the sound of his footsteps diminishing as he hurries west, runs toward the Hudson River and the docks.

I see that man standing there, against those blazing white petunias, every time I pass 21 Perry Street. Suppose we had taken the dare, suppose we had not circled the block? Maybe what happened on that first page would have happened in fact. Maybe I would have been a widow; maybe there would have been no Kate, no Mag, no memories. That I might have been the one with the knife between the shoulder blades never occurs. Like most people, most Westerners anyway, I have a sneaking suspicion I am immortal.

But why — aside from the fact that there was indeed once a man lurking in the areaway — bring so heavy an imaginative burden to so innocuous a place as the basement apartment of 21 Perry Street? Easy. That is where my life as an adult began.

St. John's Church owned a lot of property: five or six houses on West Eleventh Street and seven or eight more on Perry Street, which ran parallel. Between the two, and hidden from passersby, was perhaps the most secret of all the Village's secret gardens. It was very large, with two fountains, a small stone altar, private sitting areas at the rear of each basement apartment, a towering catalpa tree which in spring had a haunting, peppery scent, rose of Sharon bushes and spirea and a community of box turtles, invisible in winter and shy in summer. Once there had been peacocks, too, spreading their tails along the paved pathways.

All St. John's tenants had keys to the garden, and on summer Saturday afternoons B. and I would unlock an inconspicuous wooden door on Eleventh Street, carry our cheese sandwiches through the cool dark tunnel that led to the minister's small enclosure, cross it, and enter the garden, to sit for hours on the stone bench that circled the catalpa and dream about getting a basement apartment. It was hot and still in the garden — street sounds rarely penetrated — and though our butts were pocked by the bench's granular surface and our backs ached, we seldom left before sunset.

Finally a family on Perry Street moved out and we leaped, signing the lease before we even took a good look at what we were getting. The previous tenant was a set designer, with a presto-chango approach to décor. The furniture, for instance, had been spray-painted *in situ,* which meant the walls it hid were blotched with various colors. He had made a dollhouse for his daughter by building shelves in an unused fireplace. Filled, it was charming. Empty, it was a fireplace clogged with splintery boards. The kitchen stank of cats.

No matter. We scrubbed and deodorized and hung wallpaper along the kitchen's long east wall, and Jerry built bookcases in the small back room we called the study. He built bookcases in the living room, too, on either side of the fireplace, while B. hefted the shelves and handed out nails, as eager as he had been on Twenty-first Street to make himself a home.

An interior decorator could not date that apartment — B. and I were equally unwilling to enter department stores and indifferent to trends, but for our Paul McCobb couches and linen-shaded standing lamps — but I think a cultural historian could. The little foreign matchbooks came from West Fourth Street and were very Village. The Chinese export porcelain cups, each of which had at least one hairline crack and held cigarettes, were very New England, as was the white ironstone pitcher crammed, depending on the season, with chrysanthemums or laurel leaves. The Spode dinner service spoke of a trip or two to London, the copper pots in the kitchen of a trip or two to Paris, and the reproduction eighteenth-century silver-plate of an inability to afford sterling combined with a rejection of stainless steel modernism. The two wine racks in the coat closet told of someone venturing beyond Soave and Chianti, and the copies of *Tropic of Cancer, Tropic of Capricorn,* and *Les Amours Jaunes* argued junior year abroad. Almost everything from West Eleventh Street had come with us, and now we had a real Windsor chair.

In the house next door lived May Swenson, a stocky woman whose hair was cropped short over her bullet head and whom we used to see peering from her second-floor window into the garden. Justin O'Brien — "the Gide man," B. explained — had a duplex a few doors down but was seldom in residence. His Chinese cook, though, was forever getting drunk and forever setting fire to the kitchen.

A family with a lot of money moved in across the way, and when the husband made what the head of the garden commit-tee, a skinny little woman who wore high-top sneakers, per-ceived as encroachments on the community space, she chased him down West Fourth Street with the hatchet she'd been using to kill privet. The tall, Slavic-looking woman who had the floor-through above O'Brien and claimed to be a Russian prin-cess had French perfumes delivered from Bigelow's Drugstore and, seemingly unacquainted with cloth diapers, kept her young son in so many layers of disposables that one could have driven a truck between his legs.

The middle-aged woman who lived in the garden apart-ment to our right was a buyer of notions for a large department store and had never married, she told me, because everyone in her family was crazy and she did not want to pass on the taint. Al, an ex–tap dancer, and Bud, who hooked rugs, strung their terrace with fairy lights ("Ho, ho," we chortled) at Christ-mastime and gave tasteful little dinners, more tasteful even

than ours. The garden apartment next to theirs was lived in by
a former nightclub singer and girl-about-town in her late thirties who got herself knocked up by a young stranger. She
married him and promptly turned from continental layabout to
Italian mama, a switch so startling to her amiable, fat-necked
groom that he, starved for glamour, had an affair with Al.

I loved living at 21 Perry Street. Finally I could do again
what I had done for all the years of my childhood. I could spy.

My family spied. If my aunt was looking out the window
and a neighbor's car drove by, she would say, "I wonder where
the Armstrongs are going this time of day." The lights going on
next door would evoke my mother's "Guess the Tingleys are
home," and my grandmother, who spent every afternoon sitting
in her bay window, was timekeeper for the twice-weekly meetings of the woman who lived across the street and the man with
whom she was having an affair. "There goes Ralph," Ganny
would say as he turned his car into her driveway, and "There he
goes again" an hour later. But they never gossiped, not even
among themselves, nor did they want to know more than what
they had seen with their own eyes. Watching the play was
sufficient, and the house, with its two porches and big windows, gave them front seats. Small wonder that I, too, grew up
a spectator. I had spent too many hours with my grandmother
to be otherwise.

Now, instead of sitting with Ganny, with my head, like
hers, turned toward Hope Street, I walked the paths of St.
John's Garden, watching for shadows beyond the windows,
pausing to chat with whoever was sitting under the catalpa
tree. If I was not really at home with everyone, neither was I a
stranger to anyone, and if all my acquaintances were slightly
skewed, well then, so was I.

It was strange, being idle. A skinny little black man —
"dustman to the literati" we used to call him, because he worked
for a lot of Village editors — did the cleaning while I lay on the

chaise longue we had bought for the bedroom and read. I read
Dorothy Sayers and thought myself Harriet Vane, I wrote a fan
letter to John Dickson Carr, I became the self-styled "greatest
living expert" on the British working-class novel, and I argued
with B. about Salinger, whom he loved and whom I, with the
plodding Gentile's instinctive distrust of the quicksilver Jew,
found too clever by half. Once outside the house, though, I
seldom delivered an opinion. It would not have done, not with
my not having an official position in our world. The wives I
remember from dinner parties, the ones around my age, at
least, were usually silent, and those who were not talked too
much, anxious to get a word in, anxious to show that they, too,
had read Wellek and Warren. The worst of the latter were
those married to writers. Tell him you liked chapter seven in
particular and she would say, "We worked awfully hard on that
one." Eventually, "writer's wife" became the term B. and I used
for all suckerfish.

None of us had mastered charm, and the only time we saw
it was when the dinner guest was English. A visiting English
editor never had to buy a meal or a drink or pay for his own
theater ticket, nor did he ever try to. He simply opened his
mouth and let the clipped vowels roll out.

My dinner parties grew ever grander, culminating in the
evening I served beef Wellington. "*Gourmet's,*" I said, when
asked. That was how one answered culinary questions then.
Another guest, usually a woman, would raise an inquisitive
eyebrow, and the hostess would say "*Gourmet's*" or "*Dione's,*"
and, later, "*Michael's*" or "*Julia's.*" We all attempted mousse au
chocolat, we all aspired to Pavilion, and we all reveled in Joseph
Wechsberg. If we had read M. F. K. Fisher (but none of us had
yet), we would have reveled in her, too.

Who were "we"? Mostly we were bright young men and
their first wives, and now I can scarcely remember anyone's

name or face, because we were all interchangeable. What I remember better is the recipes clipped from the *Times,* because this was the age of Craig Claiborne, and copper pots from Bazar Français on Sixth Avenue, and the timid progression from an after-dinner cognac to an after-dinner marc because the latter was earthier, more real somehow. "I am measuring out my life with coffee spoons," I would say to B. when we came home from that night's dinner party, and together we would preen our feathers, serene in the belief that we spoke the same language. Certainly we shared allusions.

But what was I to do with myself? Maybe this was my chance to *write.* If I italicize the word, it is because the act was something I approached on my knees. Turning out copy and captions took only cleverness, but *writing* took — oh God, it made me nervous just to think about it. B.'s parents sent me a check for a course in short-story writing at the New School. Terrified at being put to the test, I spent the money on clothes.

I — we, really, because it was B. who invariably propelled me to action — wrote to Columbia for the graduate school catalogue. It was not too late to become the academic my father had always wanted me to be. But reading it, sprawled as always on the chaise longue, I suddenly remembered how it was to have to scrawl teeny-tiny notes — "outgrowth of Copernican cosmogony," "antithetical contradiction in metaphysical tradition" — in the margins of my anthologies, and how the late-afternoon sun caught chalk dust and suspended it in midair. I remembered how hard it was to keep one's lids from dropping over one's eyes and that I never wanted to read Thomas Hobbes again. The next day I stuck the catalogue in the wastepaper basket under the kitchen sink.

"Mees Cantwell," said Dr. Franklin, plump in his Barcelona chair. "Tell me one thing that you want." As if I knew! If I had known, I would not have been sitting in this small office, clearly the "junior" bedroom of 4½ rms., util. incl., while traffic whined on West End Avenue and other people went about their business.

Maybe it's different if you were born here. Maybe then you are deaf to the buzzing and the beating of wings. But I had come from out of town, and to me New York was a hive. You could not just live here. You had to be somebody, do something, it didn't matter what. You were not a part of the city unless you were on a bus or a subway and on your way to an office or a factory or a schoolroom. How could you know New York if you had not bolted your lunch in a coffee shop or had not had your subway stall under the East River or had not had to stand on the bus for thirty blocks because it was rush hour? You could not. The best way to know New York, to learn to love New York, was to let it wear you out. When B. came home at night, I envied him his exhaustion.

I had always assumed that someday I would have a baby. Once, when we had lived on East Twenty-first Street, we had even had a scare. At least, it was a scare for me. A doctor thought I was pregnant and insisted on a test, and over the weekend while we were waiting for the results, I stared at the ruin of my undefined ambitions and B. smiled foolishly and called me his "little seed-bearer."

By now, though, a lot of our college classmates had had children and I had taken to staring at Best & Co.'s ads for its Lilliputian Bazaar. They were of fat-cheeked babies, dream babies, like the babies in *The Blue Bird,* who toddled about heaven waiting until their names were called for the journey down to earth. When I visualized a child of my own, I visualized one of those babies. I never gave it a gender; I never even gave it a face. I simply saw myself with something to love lying swaddled in my arms.

"You may have waited too long," my gynecologist said, the same gynecologist who had told me that I must not get pregnant because I was too thin and anemic to carry a child. Now he was telling me that I probably had endometriosis, which he described as a "premature aging of the womb." I was still in my twenties. Stunned and dizzy, I wept, and he, eager to get me out of his office, called B. and told him to take me home.

We went to Europe for five weeks, but all that remains of the trip is an image of myself taking a shortcut through the food section of Fortnum & Mason on the way to our hotel, a shabby old place on Jermyn Street. It was about five o'clock, and customers were flocking the counters to buy vol-au-vents and those ghastly English gâteaux before going home to happy families. I was going to a high-ceilinged hotel room that lacked only a hanging man to perfect its décor, and nobody needed me anywhere. That my husband might have needed me was beyond imagining.

I thought I could be necessary to a child; it was impossible to believe that someone like myself had anything to offer an adult. I was sterile, mentally as well as physically, and I was sick. B. had said so. By now his "I didn't know how sick you really are" had the force of my mother's long-ago "Why can't you be like everybody else?"

When I looked into a mirror, I was surprised to find a face looking back at me. I know I was skinny, but I do not know if I had nice breasts or a flat stomach or firm thighs. But my hands I remember: the nails short and neatly filed, the only ring my wedding band, the fingers long as a spider's legs. How my husband and I complemented each other! His certainties fed my nothingness; my nothingness fed his certainties; and to this day I can find no fault in either of us. We could not help it.

At the end of the five weeks, B. was to return to New York and I was to take a month's tour of Italy. He had worked out the itinerary with a man who had lived in Rome for many years and knew each and every odd corner, right down to which doorway I should peer through for which view, and was excited for me.

What an introduction to the Italian Renaissance! What a way to improve my mind! But a few days before I was to leave, while we were still in London, I canceled the trip.

It was the cold. I was so cold if B. was not there to give me blood. Sometimes I wonder if he knew that for me, being away from him was like being severed from a transfusion tube. It is odd. I never used my married name and bristled when other people did. Alone, however, I whispered it over and over again — "Mrs. L., Mrs. L." — putting myself under its protection.

Back in New York, I applied myself to the asexual, unloving acrobatics of a woman bent on pregnancy, and once a month awoke to the same slow trickle. I would jump from the bed before the blood spotted the sheet, rummage for the Kotex on the closet shelf and the stringy elastic belt in the bureau drawer, and slide into five days of depression, watching my life drain into a boxful of sanitary napkins.

Coincidentally I saw a second gynecologist — I never again wanted to lay eyes on the first — about the recurrent cysts in my breasts. They were painful, but I could not keep my hands away from them, certain that in touching them I was touching my death. The doctor said they were unimportant, but why did I keep covering my chin?

"I guess I'm self-conscious about these pimples."

"Have you ever had acne before?"

"No."

"Are you taking any kind of medication?"

"Yes."

I described the pills the first gynecologist had given me to regulate my menstrual flow.

"Did you know they prevent conception?"

"No. He never mentioned that."

"Do you want children?"

"Oh, yes."

"Well, stop those pills and let me check you out and we'll see what happens."

The next month my period didn't arrive.

On the Saturday night of the weekend over which we waited to hear if the frog had died — "the frog died" was code then for "pregnant" — Jerry, B., and I saw *The Nun's Story* at Radio City Music Hall. "You are, you are," my husband said. "I *know* it." I knew it, too, and made B. and Jerry shield me from the crowds as we left the theater. One bump and that fertilized egg might be dislodged.

On Monday morning I called the doctor's office, and yes, the frog had died. I do not remember whether I called B. I do not remember whether we celebrated; I do not remember anything except feeling as cleansed, as scrubbed and laundered and turned inside out, as I did when, in childhood, I left the confessional. I thought God had punished me for having sealed my womb as if it were a Mason jar. But he had not. God loved me.

· 2 ·

MY FACE WAS green and nausea was constant, and before the obstetrician prescribed some little pills that were pink on one side and blue on the other, I lived on crackers and mashed potatoes and Schweppes tonic water. At night I would lie in bed fingering the small bumps that surrounded my nipples and pressing my interlaced hands just above the pubic hair to feel that minute swell. And Jerry disappeared.

No, he did not really disappear. He went back to Seattle, I think, but I am not sure, because I was blind and deaf to anything that did not have to do with my baby. There must have been a leavetaking, and probably a farewell dinner, too, but memory stops at *The Nun's Story* and his guiding hand on my elbow. So Jerry left without my noticing, on what I suppose was a summer day, while the Vermont shopkeeper we met a few months later, a gimpy little bird who said, "That's the stuff!" when B. told him I was pregnant, is stamped forever on my mind. My husband photographed me that afternoon, standing beside our tiny car, exultant, hair flying, Shetland pullover caching the tiny bulge. Our first photograph: my daughter's and mine.

Now when I lay on the chaise longue it was to unpack and pack again the little sweaters knitted by my mother-in-law and the lucky booties sent me by the old woman who lived next door to Ganny and the lacy white blanket, sweater, and cap I made for the day we brought the baby home. Each was held up, smoothed out, refolded, then laid reverently in white tissue paper and returned to the quasi-mahogany sideboard, which was once again a quasi-mahogany bureau. I read Alan Gutt-macher on babies until the book was tattered, showing B. line drawings of the fetus at four months, five months. "Now she's got fingernails," I'd say. "Now she can suck her thumb . . . has hair . . . would live if she were premature." At a cocktail party, a man told me I was the most attractive woman in the room, not remembering (though I did) that we had met a year before, when I was thin and empty and invisible.

My happiness was a blanket around our house, around B., too. The night the diaper service man came, B. marveled at the choices and was tempted by polka dots. I, matronly and self-assured, smiled fondly at my little boy, my husband, and said the plain bird's-eye would do.

She was "Michel," this dolphin that swam inside my belly, rolling and diving and kicking, because we thought the name nondefinitive, but she was really Katherine because we were sure she was a girl. Even so, it was "Michel due" — no sense in tempting fate — that I wrote in my pocket diary under March

17, amused by our baby's birthday. Papa would have laughed and sent her green carnations.

I, too, was swimming, covering the city with the slow, easy crawl with which my aunt traveled Bristol Harbor, accompanied by my baby. We would go for walks, my child and I, and converse for miles. I had always talked to myself, moving my lips and tightening my eyebrows and catching odd glances from passersby, and now I talked to her. "Look, Michel," I would say when we passed the old Northern Dispensary down on Christopher Street. "This is where Edgar Allan Poe went when he had a bad cold." And, as I settled heavily into my seat at Carnegie Hall, "Now, Michel, we're going to listen to Beethoven." My baby was safe, so safe, because she was enclosed in me, and nothing and no one could hurt her while I lived. And if I died? Well, then, we would die together and neither of us would be lonely in paradise.

Old ladies were to the left and right of me in the balcony at Carnegie Hall, old ladies who said, "Oh, that Lenny," even when Lenny wasn't conducting. To them, any dark-haired young man on the podium was Bernstein, and to me, too, who never really heard the music, only floated in the sound.

Before the concert — I had subscribed to a Friday afternoon series — I invariably lunched with Sally, a copy editor I had known at *Mademoiselle,* and caught up on the gossip in a country from which I was now very far away. *Charm,* "The Magazine for the Working Woman," had folded, and its editors had been shipped over to *Mlle.,* which meant two people for every job. C.A. had lost her chair early, to a former Hungarian baroness who, blond, blue-eyed, and zaftig, was said to look like something painted on a ceiling in Dresden. But B.T.B. was prepared to outsit everyone, and did. So was the beauty editor, the one with the nose that could slit envelopes.

"Really, Mary, you've got to have nerves of steel to survive the tension," Sally would say, and I, knowing that I did not have nerves of steel, would count myself blessed for being able to sit on Ararat and watch the flotsam and jetsam pass by. There was no place I had to be, no appointment but for the doctor's I had to keep, no demand I had to make on myself. All I had to do was be. Be, and prepare a place and a wardrobe for my baby.

Lord & Taylor would not do for a layette, being inextricably linked with the sweaters and Bermuda shorts of a girl I was beginning to forget and would not remember again for a long, long time. Saks Fifth Avenue appealed, because both my high school graduation dress and my wedding dress had come from there and I was infatuated with what seemed a sort of symmetry. But on the day I went to the children's floor, customers, too many for me to have a saleslady's undivided attention, crowded the long counters. I wanted a serious talk about undershirts and sacques and those little nightgowns that tie with a string at the bottom. I wanted to know about snowsuits.

The Lilliputian Bazaar did not live up to its newspaper advertisements — nothing could have — and in the end I wandered into Bergdorf's, where my wedding garter had come from. Here was a cushioned chair, and a perfumed hush, and a middle-aged woman who spoke of receiving blankets and terrycloth bibs and baby's little bonnets.

"You'll want at least three or four of these little sheets," she said, "and I like these little shirts that tie at the side — so much easier than pulling them over baby's head. Oh, and diaper pins. I'll bet you never even thought of diaper pins. See these, how the point is covered so that baby can't possibly be pricked, even if the pin opens by mistake? And then, of course, you'll need rubber pants. Aren't these cute?"

I was joining a club; I was learning the rules, the secret code even. I had never heard of a receiving blanket or a special pin for diapers or a little shirt that tied at the side. "See, B.?" I said when the packages, along with a bassinet, arrived from

Bergdorf's. "These shirts are much easier to use than the ones you have to pull over their heads, and the thing about these diaper pins is that they. . . ." He was as thrilled as I.

What a husband he was in those days, what a wonderful father-to-be, poring over Guttmacher, reading and rereading *Thank You, Doctor Lamaze*. If we could have, we, too, like Marjorie Karmel, would have called our doctor from the Café du Dôme in Montparnasse on a night that "was fresh and full of the smell of earth that blows over Paris on a summer night." Instead we would be calling him from a basement apartment in Greenwich Village. Never mind. Hadn't we always told ourselves, and everyone else, that living in the Village was a lot like living on the Left Bank?

I would not be able to Lamaze till the end, we figured, but surely I could do it for a few hours before caving in to twilight sleep or whatever it was they gave you. And wouldn't it be wonderful if I could spare our baby from being born drowsy! So off we went to someplace on the Upper West Side, some small, shabby room with folding chairs, to watch a film on the birth of a baby according to Lamaze.

Being there was like being in the old Needle Trades Auditorium — the same audience, mostly Jewish, with the same fierce thirst for information — and for one sick second or so I was once again waddling down the long corridor to the chair. But when the baby's head began to show, a scarcely visible darkness between the thighs of a grimacing, panting woman, I cheered like the others and exchanged shy smiles with my companions in fecundity.

My Lamaze instructor, Mrs. Bing, was, predictably, on the Upper West Side as well, in an apartment near the Museum of Natural History that was milky with light and had geraniums blooming along the windowsills. Later on, Mrs. Bing got rather famous for being a Lamaze pioneer, and when people told me they had been in one of her classes, I would let drop that I had known her when and had been tutored alone. I was boasting, of course, but I was also giving myself an excuse to recall those winter mornings and the sun scouring Mrs. Bing's uncurtained windows. "Sink contraction, not pain," she would order — her accent, like Dr. Franklin's, was faintly Germanic — and I would obey. "Huff! Now puff! Now do your *effleurage*."

I huffed, I puffed, I did my *effleurage,* brushing my hands in a circular movement over my belly, and when I got home I did it all over again. After dinner, B., my *monitrice*, would sit in the chaise longue, watch in hand, timing me while I, supine on the bed, practiced the three stages of breathing.

"Not long enough! Do it again!" I'd do it again.

"Did you do that *effleurage* right?" Yessir!

It is curious. I can see the white light and the bare floorboards in Mrs. Bing's living room, and the pots of geraniums on the windowsills, but I can no longer see the building. Which one of the big apartment houses up by the museum is it? I cannot tell. No doorway catches my eye, no trees or clumps of bushes clutch at my memory. But it is there somewhere, I know, the place where I huffed and puffed and rubbed my stomach and held my breath for . . . how many counts was it? One of those old behemoths still holds that big, high-ceilinged room, and that room still holds my joy, and if I am sad whenever I am in the neighborhood, it is because it is a cruelty to have known perfect happiness. Up there, up near the dinosaur eggs and the trumpeting elephants, I am once again that young woman with the big belly and my Kate is once again sleeping peacefully in the amniotic sac, and my heart breaks for both of us.

I awoke on March 17, waiting. "They never come when they're supposed to," I told B., and sent him off to work. All day long I waited, dusting the furniture, scrubbing the bathtub, longing for the moment when, like somebody in the movies, I would bend over, clutch my stomach with both hands, and say — to whom? I was alone — "I think it's time." Meanwhile the baby was quiet, scarcely moving, hardly even stretching her legs. I know she could hear, but could she see? Do babies keep their eyes closed until they're born? Or do they open them, look around, study the terrain?

After supper, we went to the movies. With no baby yet in view, of course we would go to the movies. We saw *Our Man in Havana*, in Times Square, where Irish and Irish-for-a-day drunks were roistering down Broadway.

The next morning, on the dot of 8:30, I felt a dull ache in my back, which was repeated about fifteen minutes later.

"The baby's coming," I said, as cool and know-it-all as I had been the day before. "But it's going to take hours, so you just go off to work." My husband, obedient to the superb creature I had become, did as he was told.

So much to do! I had to go to the A & P so that B. would have something to eat for the next few days. Then I had to pick up the slipcovers I had left at the cleaner's so the living room would look nice. Waiting for the cleaner to find them, trying to distract myself from the contractions ("Don't sink pain!" Mrs. Bing was hissing into my ear. "Sink contraction!"), I studied the little plastic bird on the counter. It kept dipping its head, up, down, up, down, toward a glass of water. *I will never forget this bird,* I said to myself. *I will never forget this moment.*

"I'm in labor, I'm in labor," I wanted to shout to the people I passed on Seventh Avenue on the walk home. "Look at me, look at me, look at how it's done!"

On my hands and knees, I crawled around the couch and loveseat, closing the snaps that held the slipcovers to the tapes sewn to their undersides. Finished! I washed every dish, did a last run with the vacuum cleaner. Finished! I ate my favorite lunch, egg salad on white. Finished! And at last I crawled onto the chaise longue with Rose Macaulay's *The Towers of Trebizond.* I loved that book. Who wouldn't love a book that began

"'Take my camel, dear,' said my aunt Dot, as she climbed down from this animal on her return from High Mass"? But after a while I could no longer rise to Macaulay's High Anglican empyrean and dialed B. "Come home," I said, still calm, still grand.

Because we thought overnight cases tacky, bourgeois, my nightgowns and toothbrush were in a paper shopping bag, along with a handful of lollipops that were supposed to provide glucose when my energy flagged during labor. Together, with B. carrying the shopping bag, we walked out the door and up Perry Street to Seventh Avenue, and together we directed a cabdriver: "Doctors Hospital."

"Doctors Hospital?" the driver said. "I hear that's some place. Jackie Gleason was just there, and they tell me the parties were *something*."

Judy Garland dried out in Doctors Hospital, I believe, and it was a nice place to go after a suicide attempt and an even nicer place to go if you were having a baby, because it had room service. Queenly in my wheelchair, I watched while B. fumbled in his wallet for his Blue Cross card. Gracious even with an enema tube dangling from my backside, I chatted with the nurse while she shaved my pubic hair, faithful to my parents' creed that small talk could raise you above anything. Because I felt the pains — oh, no, the contractions — in my back, B. and my doctor did the *effleurage* for me, circling their hands over my spine while I lay on my left side, facing a bureau and focusing on a drawer pull. Only once was there a break in my Lamaze breathing. B. had ordered a sandwich, and the crunch of the pickle he was chewing distracted me. "Stop that pickle," I said. He stopped.

"Look," the doctor said, rolling me on my back and shining a bridge lamp between my parted knees. What pleasure to lie with my legs spread, pubis shaved, blood trickling, stomach swollen, an inch or so of dark head visible in my vagina, and nothing on a man's face but love and joy.

In the labor room, or so I understood, there were rails on the beds so the maniac maternals wouldn't fall to the floor. But here I was in a wooden four-poster, while a light snow drifted past the window. The window was slightly open, and through it I could hear the faraway whine of traffic fourteen floors down on East End Avenue. Sometimes the curtain rustled; sometimes there was a footfall in the corridor. There was no other sound beyond my "Huh, huh, huh, huuuuuuh." "The baby's crowning," the doctor said to B. "Help me wheel her to the delivery room."

Something happened next, a coincidence, which would be unacceptable in fiction and is barely acceptable in fact. But for one who believed then that the mills of the gods do indeed grind, it seemed reasonable, predictable even. On the way into the delivery room, we were stopped by a doctor who said to my obstetrician, "Do you want any help, Elliott?" He did not recognize me, but I did him. He was the doctor who had said I was too frail to carry a child and medicated me with a contraceptive. "No," I replied before my doctor could open his mouth, and we sailed on.

I had imagined bright lights and white-robed, white-masked nurses flanking the table, not a small, quiet room empty except for a nurse who was putting kidney-shaped bowls in a cabinet. No matter. I needed no encouragement, no towels dabbed on the forehead, only the doctor's "Push . . . stop . . . pant . . . push . . . stop." And at last, "Here's the head . . . I've got the shoulder . . . Mary, it's a girl."

"It's Katherine," I said, and let go of the handgrips.

Dying, even if the crossover is accomplished with a fanfare of bugles and the raising of a golden curtain, cannot be so profound a shock as the birth of a child. Nothing, not all the reading, not all the line drawings, not Mrs. Bing's big card-board-mounted pictures of a baby traveling down the birth canal, had prepared me for the sight of a human being emerging from between my legs. Katherine had dark hair, two deep dimples, and was yelling.

The nurse, through finally with the kidney-shaped bowls, dried the baby with a towel, slid her into a diaper and a slightly tattered, too-big shirt, and said, "Ooh, look! She's got dimples."

"Will she keep them?"

The doctor, sitting between my knees with his head bent over a needle and thread — he was sewing up the episiotomy and looked like a tailor — laughed. So did the nurse, as she tried to hand me the baby.

"No," I said.

"Don't you want to hold her?" she asked, and again I said no.

"I might drop her."

They started laughing again but stopped abruptly, because I had started to shake. There was no controlling it; even my legs were trembling. The nurse gave up and took the baby away. I gave up, too, and closed my eyes while the doctor wheeled me back to my room and to B., who had just become a father.

"Shut the window," I said, trying to talk over what was happening to me. "Shut it. Don't let me get near it. Please, I want bed rails."

A carpenter came and nailed the window to the sill. *Ridiculous,* I thought as he hammered. *I can jump through the pane.* I heard the sound of breaking glass, felt myself hurtling with the baby in my arms, heard the splat when we hit the ground.

"Don't leave me alone. Get a nurse. Put me out."

A fat Irishwoman came and settled herself into the chair in the corner. Another doctor came in and injected something into my arm. The last thing I saw was the light and the hope fading from my husband's eyes, and the last thing I thought was that my baby, ejected now from the fortress that was myself, would never be safe again.

For years I could not think about, much less talk about, those weeks that followed my first child's birth. Now I can report, but I cannot interpret. Compulsion, depression, anxiety: I can work up a song and dance about them. Psychosis — there! I took the easy way out, I gave horror a name — is beyond analysis.

Dr. Franklin arrived the next morning. He came every morning after that and held my hand, and although I cannot remember what I said to him, I do remember that I said nothing to B., afraid that if I diverted one word from my psychiatrist I would weaken the lifeline that was slowly, and finally, beginning to connect me to him.

Besides, Dr. Franklin would not be horrified by what he was hearing, any more than he would have fainted while watching an operation. My husband, however, was not equipped to deal with sickness, or so I felt and so I still believe. If he could look into my head, I figured, he would run away. Still, my having excluded him from my madness must have seemed yet another way of excluding him from my life.

I begged my obstetrician to tie me to the bed. He would not. I begged him to move me to the psychiatric floor. He would not. How could I nurse the baby, he asked, if I were that far from the nursery? Strange. I, mad, knew what should be done. He, sane, would not do it.

One night the fat Irish nurse fell asleep in the chair and I, staring across the bed rails at her plump, pink, piggy face, panicked and woke her. "I saw on your admission form that you're a Catholic," she said. "Pray."

The hospital was full of wanderers, most of them diaper service salesmen popping up unexpectedly in one's doorway. But once a woman dispensing religious tracts slipped into my room and spilled badly printed exhortations all over my bed. She was trying to enlist me in Jehovah's Witnesses. Another time a nurse, young and pretty and so thin she scarcely left a shadow, slipped into my room and told me that nerves were the price one had to pay for being as delicately attuned, as sensitive, as we. Meanwhile the fat Irish nurse mumbled her Hail Marys and then, nodding off, as always, at midnight, left me to the devil.

When the nurse who worked the evening shift in the nursery, and who brushed Katherine's hair into different dos — sometimes parted down the side, sometimes down the center — brought her to me for a feeding, I would not let her leave, because the old Irishwoman ran off down the hall then to her cronies, leaving me free to crash the window with my beautiful, innocent baby in my arms. Early one morning, when the Irishwoman left to get my orange juice, I got out of bed and baptized my daughter with water from the lavatory faucet. At least she would go without original sin.

Friends came to visit. I smiled, I chatted, and if any of them wondered why there were rails on my bed, they never did so aloud. B. came every night, stopping first at the nursery to peer through the glass at his daughter, and told me who had called, who had written, what his parents had said, who had invited him for dinner. When my breasts swelled to blue-veined white globes — "You've got enough milk to feed every kid in the nursery," the night nurse crowed — he arrived, unasked, with nursing bras. "Size 40C," he said proudly, taking my abundance for his own.

"If you'll just let me out of here, away from this window," I said to my doctor, "I'll be all right." So he released me from the hospital a day early, and back I went to our basement apartment, frantic to feel nothing but Manhattan underfoot. But first we watched while the nurse dressed our child in the clothes B. had brought from home, gasping when she broke off the withered stub of the umbilical cord. Then she swaddled Katherine in the lacy knitted blanket and stuck the lucky booties on her feet and handed her to B., who smiled to see his baby, his lamb, in his arms.

Just as I had thought overnight cases bourgeois, so I thought a baby nurse a sinful self-indulgence. So I had asked our cleaning woman, Mamie, who claimed some acquaintance with infant care, to come in for a few hours every day for the week after I came home from the hospital. She came once, then never again, and when chided by a neighbor said cheerfully, "You know me, Miz Gibney. Can't handle responsibility."

For two days I sat alone, holding the baby until B. came home from work, afraid that if I put her down for more than a minute, she would stop breathing. I nursed her, too, although my nipples were cracked and bleeding, because I was afraid I would make mistakes with a formula. On the third day Hoppy, a practical nurse, arrived.

Hoppy was Jamaican, short and round and brown, and when she walked, her starched white uniform crackled and her spotless white shoes squeaked. She slung Katherine over her shoulder, rather like a dishrag, and commandeered the apartment, whistling or singing ("You've got to get them used to noise") as she moved from room to room. When Hoppy swaddled Katherine in a receiving blanket, it was because she "needs the comfort"; when she made me nurse the baby every time she cried, hungry or no, it was because she "needs the comfort"; when she asked Katherine, "Do they speak Latin where you come from?" I knew that like me, she believed in a room up in heaven where babies waited to be called to earth. When Hoppy was there, my daughter was safe, and until the night B. told me about Lewis, so was I.

Lewis, the first child of another editor and his wife, was four weeks old. "Kate's got a date for the junior prom," his father said when Katherine was born, and he sent her a split of champagne in his son's name. A few days before her birth, we had had dinner at their house and I had given Lewis his bottle, "for practice," his mother had said. Now he was dead, B. said, with tears in his eyes, and he had not wanted to tell me but had to for fear I might call Lewis's mother one bright morning and say, "How is Lewis? How are his burps?"

There were tears in my eyes, too, but Hoppy said, "No, no, Mrs. L., you'll spoil the baby's milk if you cry." So I didn't cry, and wondered if there had been something wrong in the way I had held the bottle.

That night, lying beside my daughter, whose bassinet I had put next to the bed so I could listen to her breathing, my right hand holding down my left so that I could not close them around the tiny neck and squeeze, I resolved that whenever I felt the urge to kill someone, I would redirect it and kill myself instead. The relief was tremendous.

Many nights I slept on the living room couch, leaving my husband alone in the bedroom with Kate. She was safe with him. Often I would stare at the tiny, pulsing fontanel, thinking of how easily my long strong thumb could crush it. Her neck was so little one hand could break it. I would not bathe her. My husband did. He thought I was afraid she would slip. I was afraid I would push. But every time I felt my hands moving or realized that my eyes had been too long on her neck, her head, I determined again to harm myself before I could harm her. The decision to die is a great restorative.

After six weeks the sickness trailed away, dispersing in shreds, like clouds lifting. The fear of heights did not. Day after day Dr. Franklin stood me next to his twelfth-story window, put both his arms around me so I would feel secure, and said, "Tell me what you see."

"There's a man with a raincoat and a shopping bag, and I can see a woman pushing a baby carriage. There's a little girl crossing the street, and three cabs at the corner." Naming. I kept naming things, people, eventually emotions, and the naming gave order to chaos.

But the fear of heights — ah, the fear of heights. Even today I stay away from windows on high floors, and when circumstances push me onto terraces, I sidle along the walls, my fingers looking for crevices among the bricks. It never leaves me, that reminder that once upon a time I was crazy.

· 3 ·

THE FIRST TIME I took Katherine on an outing, on a Sunday afternoon in May when she was six weeks old, the wheel came off her green plaid baby carriage. A garage mechanic repaired it — "On the house, lady," he said — and set me, grinning, back on West Tenth Street. There could have been no stronger line of demarcation between me and those people up on the Upper East Side, I thought, infatuated with my fecklessness, than the distance between a fabric carriage with dodgy wheels and a Silver Cross pram. Actually, B. might have preferred a Silver Cross pram, but it would not have gone with the new identity I was coining for myself: Village mother.

That day and many days thereafter I took my daughter to Washington Square, to the southeast corner, where a big sycamore that I came to call the baby tree spread its branches over a large, grubby sandpit. A certain kind of Village mother spent hours there, offering chunks of raw potato to her teething child. The purest example (all struck me as variations on a type) was a sallow, stringy-haired young woman who, talking constantly, made much of her Jewishness and her husband's blackness. She brandished his color, in fact, as if it were a flag. Meanwhile the baby, scrawny and dun-skinned, was treated with the rough affection due a puppy. But then, rough affection — dumping one's offspring in its carriage, carrying it more or less upside down on one's hip — was, like the raw-potato teething tool, a function of Village style.

I would have loved to talk to someone, especially about Beechnut's as compared to Gerber's and whether pacifiers made for buckteeth, but I was too shy to start a conversation, and nobody was inclined to start one with me, probably because my face is stony in repose, and forbidding. Still, it was pleasant under the baby tree — the drunks mostly clustered by the fountain, and the folksingers who preceded the drug dealers hadn't yet arrived — and membership in the club to which I had so desperately wanted to belong was glorious.

About four o'clock, about the time the air began to turn blue, I would rise from the bench and kick up the carriage brake and off we would go, past the stern, beautiful houses that were all that was left of Catherine Sloper's Washington Square to Bleecker Street, where strolled another kind of Village mother. This one pushed an enormous perambulator in which lay, banked in pillows and laces and fleecy wools, a fat little boy who was almost always named Anthony. I know this because a silver tag on a chain, reminiscent of the kind that drapes decanters, invariably swagged his coverlet. There it was, inscribed for all to see: ANTHONY.

Lucky Anthony, to be going home to a crowd. Like a lot of people with small families and without a strong ethnic identity, I thought the spirits were higher and the sentiments warmer in big Italian and Jewish households. Not in B.'s Jewish household — he had never even had a bar mitzvah, and if his parents knew a word of Yiddish, I never heard it — but in the kind I had glimpsed in old photographs of tenement life. Snug as bugs in a rug those families were. I couldn't see the poverty for the coziness.

So when I saw Anthony after Anthony moving like Cleopatra on her barge through the dusk of late afternoon on Bleecker Street, I saw their grandparents and their aunts and uncles and cousins lined up to greet them. I saw first communions and weddings and funerals at Our Lady of Pompeii, and statues of saints dressed in dollar bills, and a network of Philomenas and Angelas and Roses stretched over the whole South Village. I envied Anthony all of them, for Katherine's sake. For my sake, too.

My mother, who was forever reminding me that she personally had scrubbed my every diaper and strained my every beet, was nonetheless rich in household help — her mother and her sister and her widowed great-aunt — and when she had walked uptown with me, it had been "Good afternoon" and "Is she teething yet?" all the way. But these were strangers on the streets of Greenwich Village, and I, who had never lost my provincial chattiness, had only an infant to talk to. "Okay," I would say as I turned the carriage into Ottomanelli's meat market, "this is where we get the veal scaloppini for Daddy and me. And you, you're having cereal and banana."

Once I had wrestled the carriage into the areaway of 21 Perry Street, however, the miracle overtook me, the miracle that always overtook me when I unlocked the door to my own home. The stove, its pilot light like a votive candle, was waiting; the refrigerator was purring; the turn of a faucet would set a pot to filling. "Poor Butterfly, though your heart is breaking," I sang while I settled Katherine into her baby butler; "The most beautiful girl in the world," while I maneuvered her small silver spoon into her small stubborn mouth; "Bye Bye, Blackbird" as, one hand firm under her rubber-pantied rump, I waltzed her to her crib.

While I wished that my father had lived to see his grandchild, I no longer felt the curious pain — a strange, slow tearing-apart — that had crossed my chest whenever I thought of him. I gave up the hope, too, never quite lost, that someday he would walk into the room. And, blessedly, a recurring dream gave up on me: a dream in which I met him, in one of his Brooks Brothers suits and a felt fedora, walking down Fifth Avenue.

"Papa!" I said. "You're alive!"

"Yes, I am, Mary Lee, but you must never tell anyone or try to find me, because if you do, I will die." So I left him in the middle of a crowd on Fifth Avenue and woke up crying.

"But Mary," a friend said once, "your father *can't* have been flawless."

"He was till I was twenty," I replied.

Perhaps if he had lived just a little longer, it might have been long enough for me to have grown away from him. But he did not, so I am forever the daughter looking for the lap that disappeared. It is the same with Katherine. If I had not gone back to work, if I had been locked up with her until the morning she left for kindergarten, I might one day have seen her as distinct from me. But I did go back, before she could even talk, and so I retain an image of my baby and myself nestled into each other like a pair of *matryoshka* dolls. She is perfect; so am I.

"Sidney," B. said, naming the owner of a small publishing house, "needs someone to read for him." "Sterling," naming a literary agent who was striking out on his own, "needs a reader." "Jack at Coward-McCann," naming an editor at a large publishing house, "needs someone to look at this and see if it can be salvaged." The manuscripts stacked beside the chaise longue, between it and the playpen, constituted the slush pile, the over-the-transom stuff, the stuff that people like me were hired, for next to nothing, to skim through. Only two — a novel and a curious little biography of a bat, both of which had been published earlier in England — were worth consideration. But I read everything, all the way through, remembering Yeats's "Tread softly because you tread on my dreams."

One woman had written a biography of Ruth Chatterton, based on clippings from old movie magazines and a brief dressing-room how-do-you-do when Chatterton was touring and played in her town. I saw it three times — she had submitted it to each of the people for whom I was working — and there cannot have been a publisher's reader in the city who had not seen it once. In truth, every publisher's reader in the city had probably seen all the manuscripts beside the chaise longue. If, working on a magazine again in years to come, I was to defend the reading of the slush pile, it was not because I believed it hid a gem. It was because I thought its originators were owed the courtesy. Most of them, after all, were not trying to get rich. They were simply trying to join a church. It was a church I had thought of joining once, but no more. Better to do what I was doing now: read in the morning light and watch my Katie roll over, stand up, spit up. We kept her crib in our bedroom until she was a year old, unable to give up the sight that greeted us when we woke. At dawn her starfish hands grasped the bars, she struggled upward, and her face appeared, like the sun rising.

Several days a month I lugged the manuscripts uptown in shopping bags, taking the bus because I was not about to spend money on cabs, and curiously nervous about crossing Fourteenth Street. Uptown, I told B. — taking my allusion, as usual, from my reading — was the world of telegrams and anger. It was also a world in which we went to a lot of cocktail parties on hot summer nights. Cold winter nights, too, I suppose, but I do not remember those. I remember the summer parties, though, because usually I was the only wife (the rest were in Amagansett with their children) among a flock of pretty young women, many of whom were sleeping with the young editors whose wives were in Amagansett. The pretty young women were in publishing, too, often fresh out of Radcliffe's summer course, and I have sometimes wondered what happened to them. They came along a bit too early for publishing houses to place them anywhere but in their textbook departments, and a bit too early for the young editors, too, who did not acquire their second wives until ten or so years later. But whatever became of them, I am sure they remained good sports, just as I am sure that none of them, to this day, would leave the milk bottle on the kitchen table.

I remember a summer Saturday afternoon, too, when we rented a car and drove to Westport for lunch with Sheilah Graham. Sheilah was a Hollywood gossip columnist whose affair with F. Scott Fitzgerald had lent her a certain literary shine, and B. was her editor. She was plump and blond and blue-eyed, the kind of woman who looks as edible as a bonbon, and when Katherine was born she had given her a pleated nylon bedjacket. *So Hollywood,* I thought, and tied it round the baby's tiny shoulders whenever we had dinner guests.

Sheilah made me laugh — she was sharp as a needle — and never more so than that afternoon. Katherine was in her infant seat, on the kitchen table, when Sheilah called her teenage son in to see her. "Fair warning, Rob," she said, pointing at Kate. "The wages of sin."

But there was no sin in Katherine's conception: a judge had sanctioned it. Rather than being the restriction I had feared, marriage had turned out to be roomy. It allowed for all sorts of stuff. Except, of course, for flirtations. When a young man who had not noticed my wedding ring spoke of seeing me again — we were at a cocktail party — I backed away as if presented with a snake. "Lock Mary Lee into an igloo with Mastroianni for two years," B. boasted once, "and *nothing* would happen." At least, I thought he was boasting.

I remember something else as well, the nights when Katherine squalled and condemned me to blurred and stumbling walks around the living room. I remember a paperbound copy of Dr. Spock hurled against a wall, the spine splintering on

impact and the pages cascading to the floor. I remember thinking I would do anything for sleep. And because of all that, I
remember Bloomingdale's as I would paradise.

There was a morning when I was tired, so tired I was
having dizzy spells. *I'll faint,* I told myself, *and something terrible will happen to the baby. She'll catch her head between the
crib bars or pull herself over them and fall. Or she'll stop breathing, like little Lewis did, because I am not watching. If I take my
eyes off her, she will die. But I am going to take my eyes off her,
because I cannot keep them open.*

We seldom had a babysitter unless we were going to the
movies or to someone's house for dinner. But the woman who
usually cared for Katherine then was home, thank God, and
free. I was dizzy until the moment she walked into the kitchen,
all white uniform and rubber-soled Oxfords and competence. I
was about to say, "If you could just watch Katherine while I
nap" when my head cleared and exhaustion dropped from my
shoulders. I would go to Bloomingdale's instead. I would look
at the model rooms.

I have never known the name of a plant that has long
stems and round leaves and that, dried, smells of spices and
pepper. Antique dealers love it. So do the owners of "country"
shops. But Bloomingdale's was the first place I ever smelled
those leaves. Smell them now and I have just traversed the
Directional couches and the rosewood room dividers to join
the shoppers who, barred from entrance by a velvet rope, are
viewing the model rooms.

Even when they were supposed to evoke the South of
France or a corner of Tuscany or somebody's Maine hideaway,
the model rooms evoked New York. It was their scale and their
extravagance and sometimes the sheer nonsense of them. All I
ever bought at Bloomingdale's, besides white-sale linens, were
lamps with black paper shades and cheeses from the delicacy
department, but I returned again and again to those rooms.

None of them, really, were to my sober, strait-laced taste. Still, I was proud of them, even proprietary. "You don't see raisin bread like this at home," a visiting friend of my mother's said one day when I gave her tea and toast. You didn't see rooms like these, either.

Once in a while a salesman would unhook the rope and escort a customer inside. The customer was always a woman, always thin, always ash blond, and almost always, I assumed, from out of town. She and the salesman would pause over a fruitwood armoire, a terra-cotta urn deep enough to hide a thief, an enormous Rya rug. He would whip out his order book; the viewers' eyes would shift to the right, where a discreet sheet of plastic-covered paper listing items and prices hung on the wall. God! That woman had just spent $500 on — oh, let's say a beaten copper tray from Morocco.

Together they emerged, the woman flushed with the pride of someone who can spend $500 on foolishness, the salesman saying something about delivery in ten days. The line of viewers parted to let them through, then moved slowly on to the next room. No one spoke; we were too busy inhaling opulence.

Dreamily I would descend the escalators and eventually the stairs to the basement. Lackadaisically I would make my way to the subway and the Fourteenth Street stop of the West Side IRT. Emerging at Twelfth Street and Seventh Avenue, I was still sedated — by the scent of the dried round leaves and the rip-rip-rip of sales slips being torn from order books. A few blocks south, a few yards west, and I was unhooking the gate into the areaway, as refreshed as if I had been hours in deep sleep. I had not spent a cent. I had not wanted to. The bustle was sufficient, and the traffic and the noise, and above all the Lethe that was Bloomingdale's fifth floor.

The rooms I thought of, still think of, as my kind of rooms I never saw. But I know where they were. They were in one, or maybe all, of five houses that stood on the corner of Greenwich Street and Dey Street in 1810. The first, at the left, is white clapboard with two dormer windows, green shutters, and a Dutch door, on the bottom half of which a man and a woman are leaning their elbows. Next to it is a brick house, much bigger and grander, with a rail-backed bench on either side of the front door. A boy is sitting on one of them.

The remaining houses are on Dey Street. The one at the corner, which is also brick, is big and grand indeed and has two entrances. Maybe the second — two men are standing on its steps — is for servants. But the one next to it, and the one beyond that, both of them white clapboard and comparatively modest, also have two entrances. So I am confused. It is a winter day, though, I am sure of that, because the trees are naked, and the sky is the same dull gray I wake up to on January mornings in New York.

But the rooms? What do I know of these rooms, some of which are shuttered? Nothing, really, only that they are spare and clean and that they have wide floorboards and small fireplaces. These are the rooms in which I have always wanted to live, the material equivalent of Jane Austen's prose, and that they once existed in Greenwich Village is reason enough for me to believe that some of them still do. Up and down the narrow streets and all the way down toward what was later called SoHo we would go, Kate in her carriage or, later, her stroller and me in my pants and sneakers. Sometimes I could see the outline of a pitched-roof house on the bigger, newer building that had stood next door and survived it. I saw boarded-up dormer windows, too, and incised stone lintels crumbling before my very eyes.

Nothing of those five houses, however, remained at the corner of Greenwich Street and Dey Street. I had been there with Jerry long before I had bought a print of that 1810 watercolor at the New York Public Library's gift counter, for plants for the windowboxes at 224 West Eleventh. The nurseries that were there then, though, are now as vanished as those five houses, and I suppose that whatever is there now will have vanished in another few decades, too. Fix it before it disappears! Fix it before it disappears! I knew I was never going to live in those rooms. I knew I was never going to find more than their traces. But what I could find I would fix, so that one day I could walk those streets again whether they had lasted or not.

I have fixed Kate and me, too, on our long late-afternoon strolls along the western shores of Greenwich Village. The boat horns — one does not hear those anymore — are lowing, and the police are riding their horses to the stables (they are vanished, too) on West Twelfth Street, and the three old musicians — Italians from the South Village, I think — who used to play songs like "Deep Purple" for change thrown from Village windows are just starting out for their evening tour.

It is time to go indoors, time to get under a roof, time for the cereal and the banana, the bath and the waltz round the living room, and if I speak as if we, too, have vanished, it is because we have. Never again would I be Kate's alone, nor would Kate be mine alone, because when she was eighteen months old I went back to work. For me to do that, she had to be born again, into another woman's care, and I had to be born again, too, to become someone who was not wholly, solely a mother. The Kate who is here now is not the Kate who was there at the beginning. That one is still in a stroller, being pushed along Hudson Street. And the woman who pushed her is still gripping the stroller's handles, still looking for rooms that are as clean and spare as a bone.

· 4 ·

I AM NOT really sure what it was that drove me back to work, although I think loneliness was part of it. Except for when I was talking to Katherine — "That's a good girl" and "Let Mommy button up Katie's sweater" — I kept a Trappist's silence. Mostly, though, it was probably pragmatism, pragmatism and a need to own New York as surely as I had owned the town in which I was raised.

I had not spent all those days in classrooms and all those nights with John Donne so that I could spend my time washing Kate's little shirts and nightgowns and hanging them on the bathroom shower rail, separating B.'s shirts (they went to the cleaner at the corner) from the sheets and towels (they went to a big pick-up-and-deliver commercial laundry), and waiting for the diaper service man. Of course not. Somebody else could do that stuff. Why should I?

Besides, I knew a man who would do the heavy cleaning. And Nanny Schaefer, who babysat for us, was tired of working out of an agency and was happy to have a regular morning job. Maybe if it had not been so easy to walk out the door, I might have stayed at home. But if I had, I would have been unhappy, and not simply because a college education was going down a drain. To live in New York, to be part of New York, I had to work.

In Bristol, I had joined the Girl Scouts and sold their cookies door to door. I had stood in our high school gymnasium wearing a blue bloomer suit and waving Indian clubs at the crowd in the bleachers. But not because I believed in the truth of scouting or the virtue of exercise. It was because I wanted to weave my life with the town's life. Traveling, I have spent more time in street markets and butcher shops than I have in museums and churches, and have imagined myself behind every closed door I have ever seen. Home with, say, a cold, I watch the five o'clock news and regret that I have not been out on the street that day to see the traffic jam at Times Square, the arrest at Grand Central. I had to work, because to someone who comes from out of town, that is what New York is for, and what it is. No matter how late at night I open my window, I can hear the streets and the sky and the buildings emitting a dull, constant drone. The hive, whatever the hour, is always buzzing.

But what should I do? I envy those for whom the world holds infinite potential, who are as flexible as whips. Except for a few weeks or so when I was ten and wanted to be an archaeologist (a few thrusts with a spade, I believed, were all it took to bring up glory), I have never wanted to be anyplace but around words. My father's cousin was a critic for the *Providence Journal;* her house burst with books piled on tables, sitting two rows deep on shelves, lining the staircase to the second floor. Papa and I thought she lived at the heart of light.

The reading I did in the chaise longue, though, was as near as I wanted to come to book publishing, and a part-time job at the Washington Square Bookstore — sweet little lending library, nice customers, lots of time for browsing — would not pay Nanny Schaefer's salary. So, fearful lest she remember that three years before I had left *Vogue* in disgrace, I made an appointment with the former gym teacher who was personnel director at Condé Nast.

"Welcome home," she caroled when I went in the door. No matter that I had walked out without giving notice, no matter at all. Half the people who had worked for Allene, she implied, had done the same. But that was what you had to deal with when you dealt with the creative. They had . . . quirks. The gym teacher smiled, serene in the knowledge that she had no quirks whatsoever.

"Now, Mary," she asked. "What have you been up to?"

"Well, I have a baby. Katherine. She's eighteen months old now, and I've been thinking that maybe there was something here I could do part-time."

"As a matter of fact, there is," she said. "Do you think you could do your old job at *Mademoiselle* in half the time?"

Of course I could, and at half the pay, too.

Among the women I worked with on fashion magazines when I was young, there must have been one who was shrewd about her salary. But I never knew her. We took it for granted that the people who worked in the art department had higher starting salaries than the rest of us, because they, having gone to art school, were presumed to have skills. We also took it for granted that the women who worked in merchandising and the men who were space salesmen made more money than we did. A successful store promotion or a few new advertising pages were evidence of their worth. But there was no way we traffickers in taste could prove our value, so most of us didn't even try. "We *never* match salaries to keep people who get another offer," the former gym teacher would say to someone who proposed to jump ship for, say, *The Ladies' Home Journal,* and — although she didn't say this bit aloud — "we never take them back."

Mademoiselle, which had been bought by Condé Nast, had not yet moved its offices to the Graybar Building, so I met C.A.'s successor, the ex-Hungarian baroness, at 575 Madison. Nothing had changed. B.T.B. was still holding court in her boudoir, the fashion editors were still wearing Italian shoes, the writers in the college and career department were still peppy. There were a few new faces — the editors from *Charm* who had succeeded in edging the editors from *Mlle.* off their chairs — and some of the old faces looked up from their desks and waved as I passed by. Before I was ten paces down the corridor, somebody told me the baroness didn't wear underwear. Somebody on a phone in the fashion department was telling one of the photographers — they were all out on college campuses photographing the August issue — that it wasn't possible that *everybody* at Wheaton had acne. Somebody else was telling Leo Lerman, in his lair and surrounded by the usual acolytes, that Mr. Capote was on the line. I was indeed home.

"There's just one thing," I told the baroness after she said she would be only too happy to have me join the copy department. "I have to go to Paris first."

Now *that* was the kind of excuse a former baroness and former editor of *Harper's Bazaar* found acceptable for almost anything. "My dear," she said in her whiskey baritone, "of course you do." Happy day! Happy Mary! Back in the lobby, the same lobby in which eight years before I had stood clutching my mother's old handbag, I said to myself, "I will never leave this again." I did not mean *Mademoiselle.* I meant work.

But if I had lived in Paris? Oh, if I had lived in Paris, I would have sat all day in cafés drinking citrons pressés and staring at passersby. I would have walked up and down those pearl-gray streets, stopping only to lean my elbows on the parapet of the occasional bridge and watch the *bâteaux mouches* slide by. On a night when B. and I were standing on the Pont Neuf, one slid by empty of passengers and sounding of "Jesu, Joy of Man's Desiring" from, I suppose, a record player. How I remember that night, that encapsulation of everything I loved most about this world: that there was a city like Paris and a composer like Bach and that I had been lucky enough to have married someone who had introduced me to both.

We all went to Paris, all the time, B. and I and our friends, clutching the clips of Craig Claiborne's most recent tour of France and lists of boutiques and the addresses of Baccarat's factory salesroom and the best perfume discounter. I could not write about New York if I were not to write about Paris as well, because Paris was what we, our crowd, wanted New York to be.

If we longed for sidewalk cafés, it was because we'd sat in them in Paris, and if we were forever lugging boughs of mountain laurel from the florist down on Greenwich Avenue to our walk-ups, it was because they were the closest thing to the bouquets we had found on every Paris corner and lugged to our hotels. We dared the nasty salesladies at Guerlain, and we bought copper pots at Les Halles, and whenever we returned home, it was with the name of a new shop or a new restaurant to pass on.

"There's this place," we'd say, "Chez l'Ami Louis. It's in an area with a lot of laundries, stuff like that, and you have to call a cab before you leave, because you'll never find one otherwise. They do this little leg of lamb. . . ." Or "Go to the Monoprix, or maybe it's the Prisunic. Anyway, it's on the Boul Mich. They have these knives and forks with plastic handles in *wonderful* colors. . . ."

In Paris I bought a present for Allie's first child (she had married an Irish Catholic from Boston, and the wedding reception, at the Plaza, was a meld of flamboyant Irish toasts and her relatives' high-nosed "Hear, hear"s), a little boy for whom I got a striped bikini. Where but in Paris could you find a bikini for an infant, or a woven straw crib lined with ruffles and flourishes? And what better place to conceive my next daughter? That B. and I might have a son was past imagining. He, like my father, was meant to sire girls.

"Don't you think we ought to quit while we're ahead?" he said, as cautious as those acquaintances — invariably Jews streaked with pessimism — who had warned me that in knitting little sweaters and assembling a layette before Katherine was born, I was thumbing my nose at the Fates. Then he warmed to the romance of it all. We would be able to tell our next child that she had come into being in the city of Notre-Dame and the Sorbonne and La Tour d'Argent.

When our first child, our Katherine, was born, we took her

to Bristol to introduce her to my grandmother. Ganny was sitting on her porch, I remember, and held out her arms for her great-grandchild. She examined her closely, running her fat little hands over Katie's honey-colored hair, poking a finger into one of her deep dimples. Then she turned the baby so that her profile was on a line with the railing.

"What on earth are you doing?" I asked.

"I just wanted to see her nose."

"What made you think she'd have a big nose?" I said, pretending I couldn't guess.

"Because," Ganny said soberly, "that's the mark the Lord set on them."

My grandmother wasn't anti-Semitic, I knew that. But I also knew that she saw all children as compendiums of those who had gone before them. I had my father's hands; my sister had my mother's; my aunt was the dead spit, she told me, of an aunt on Ganny's side, just as my mother was the dead spit of Aunt Mame, on Gampa's side. Those were the marks — an ancestor's cheekbones, the narrow Cantwell foot — the Lord set on us. But the Lord had stamped my daughter not with a beak but with a button, and now I would have another button-nose, to relieve me of the strain of loving the first one so much. Having to stretch love to cover two children would, I thought, thin it out, make it bearable.

So we went to Paris, to a room on the top floor of the Hotel Bisson, which we had read about in Liebling or Wechsberg or whoever it was that we and our fellow Francophiles were passing around those days. B. was excited by my new sexual sophistication, or, rather, carelessness: the swagger with which I had tossed out my diaphragm, my no-nonsense, knees-up, pelvis-tipped style in bed. Sex was okay now, because now I knew what it was for.

I did not get pregnant in Paris. "Next month," I said to B., having proof in Katherine that we were capable of launching legions on the world. "Both of us had rotten colds, and we had to climb four flights of stairs to our room! What can you expect?"

A few weeks later, in New York, the colds cured themselves, the egg dropped, the sperm swam, and off I went to my new job. No matter that in nine months I would have to take a few weeks off for childbirth. A pregnant editor was a commonplace at *Mademoiselle,* trundling her belly in and out of meetings, saving up her vacation days so she would get paid for the few weeks she was home with a newborn. The "office babies," we called our progeny, and today, when some of them are parents themselves, some are disappointments, and several are tragedies, we still do.

The sportswear editor, a thin young woman with a narrow fox face, is going through a rack. "It'll be shipped shorter than it is here, and it comes in a myriad of colors." That is the invariable ending of her presentation of the pick of her market: "It comes in a myriad of colors."

"Would you *look* at those buttons!" screeches the fabric editor, whose hair is a kind of Seven Sisters pageboy (though she herself dropped out of someplace on Long Island) moored with a silver barrette. "Those buttons are *impossible!*"

"Listen, it's the best thing on the line, and I think it'll photograph okay." The dress editor is using a code which all of us understand. We have to show something from this manufacturer because he advertises, and this is his most inoffensive garment.

"Well," one or two or three of us say, because this is the prescribed response to the ghastly, "it's a look."

The room is windowless, the table is littered with packs of Cheez Doodles, the smoke from a dozen or so cigarettes rises to the ceiling. The fashion department is holding its monthly meeting, and I, being a copywriter, am sitting in. B.T.B. is sitting in, too, but only for an hour or so. Other duties call, among them her punctilious red-penciled reading of copy and manuscripts (she is quite possibly the world's greatest copy editor) and the correspondence entailed by her membership in the Women's Republican Club.

The sportswear editor holds up a silver evening sweater. Everybody likes it. "Group order," somebody says. "Group order, group order!" Ten or so of us are going to get it wholesale, that's what that means. But not me. I couldn't pull that sweater over my bulge. No matter. I will participate in plenty of group orders before my time is up at *Mlle.*, or "Millie!" as B.T.B. is forever sighing. "Such a silly name."

The first editor-in-chief of this magazine lasted only a few months; by the time B.T.B. is retired, she will have lasted nearly forty years. "Dearly Beloved Family" is how she addresses the staff in the long letters she writes to us during her annual holiday in the Grand Caymans. The morning after her beet-faced, Old New York husband's sudden death, she came to the office and sat at her desk, a red pencil in her hand. Nobody interrupted her: we knew she was holding a wake in what was more surely her home than the big apartment on upper Fifth Avenue in which, we still believed, her housekeeper ironed her stockings every morning.

I have been in this meeting long enough for my eyes to water and my feet to fall asleep. Soon after B.T.B. leaves, I leave, too, for the shoebox I share with a woman who is even more pregnant than I. Short and fat, her eyes gray behind big glasses, she is a poet and playwright. Like half the people at *Mademoiselle,* she aspires to other things.

"Do you *believe* those ruffles? And would you check out those buttons?" The fabric editor is at it again; the laughter and "a myriad of colors" are crossing the hall and seeping into my office. The baroness's assistant sticks her head in my door. "I may go mad," she says, and withdraws it.

Now there is no C.A. to order the troops, and B.T.B.,

whose faith in her staff is beyond sublime, asks only that we stay out of jail. Leo Lerman is in the doorway. Do I have time for Schrafft's before going home? It is drizzling slightly, so as we leave the Graybar he knots the four corners of his handkerchief and places it on his bald head. Down the street we go, Leo either oblivious to or shrewdly aware of — i have never quite decided which — the sight he is making. I am laughing; I am always laughing. This is the season of my content.

A night in April. We are dressing for a dinner party, I in a black skirt with a porthole over which I have dropped an empire-waisted blue *schmatte. Schmatte,* along with "merch" for merchandise and "matchy-matchy," as in "That sweater and skirt are too matchy-matchy," is among the words I have picked up at *Mlle.* I have resisted pronouncing beige "behj" and kimono "kimina," but on the whole I am beginning to sound like a fashion maven. My transformation, however, is not yet complete. It is years before I discover that "maven" is Yiddish.

The dinner party is on the Upper West Side, and it is safe to say we will be eating boeuf bourguignon. It is also safe to say that after coffee, somebody will put Chubby Checker on the record player and everyone will start twisting. Everyone, that is, but me, who has learned how — "Make believe," I was instructed, "that you're drying your backside with a towel" — but who is considered (though not by me) to be *hors de combat* on account of pregnancy.

This is all anybody does after dinner parties anymore: twist. Conversation among the literati (I, of course, am not one, but B. is) has been suspended for the next two years.

To the right of the kitchen sink in the house in which I live now is a menu, slightly stained, in a narrow brown frame. "A la Halte de l'Eperon," it says at the top, beside a drawing of a duck on a platter staring fearfully at a carving knife. It's the menu for "10 mai 1962" at a restaurant called Chez Allard, and by now it has hung on the walls of four apartments. May 10 was my birthday, my second child was two months from being born, and once more we were in Paris, where, too pregnant to wander alone through Venice, as I had first planned, I was making believe I lived by taking cooking lessons from Julia Child's coauthors, Mesdames Bertholle and Beck. Every morning I took a bus up to just beyond L'Etoile, climbed a flight of stairs, tied on an apron, and, standing in a small, simple kitchen, realized the dreams of everyone who had ever read *Mastering the Art of French Cooking.*

As usual, our stay in Paris would in memory have mythic proportions, because we would have spent time with Alice B. Toklas. Alice was very real to us, especially to B., but she was also someone who had another reality, in the pages of a book. At this point the two Alices seemed one, but I have always wondered whether the Alice we knew was not the Alice Gertrude had known but the Alice Gertrude had invented.

B. wanted Alice to write her own autobiography, and a few years earlier, before I had had Kate, she had granted him an audience. She lived on the rue Christine then, in a house behind a tall wooden door that was approached through a shabby courtyard. "G. Stein, *ecrivain*" was the name above the doorbell, although Gertrude Stein had been dead for at least ten years (I seem to remember that she was still listed in the Paris phonebook, too), but there was no answer when we pushed that bell or the one beside the door to her flat.

Remembering that someone had told him Alice was slightly deaf, B. ran off to find a kiosk — he knew she could hear a telephone's ring — leaving me to stand on the stair landing, staring down at the courtyard. Suddenly the door to the right of the window opened, and there she stood, "a tiny, hunched woman with dark hair, round glasses, and a Boston voice," I wrote in my travel diary. "Deaf, closes her eyes when she laughs."

Alice asked me if I was Mrs. L. I explained that my husband was in a phone box, and she ushered me down a long dark passageway paved with Picassos. I gasped. I had not known, or perhaps I had forgotten, that these were Alice Toklas's property now.

They were hung in no particular order; some were framed, some were not, and when I paused in front of a portrait of a naked young girl holding a bunch of red roses and said, "How beautiful," Alice said, "That was the first Picasso Gertrude ever bought."

I felt like the publisher-lodger in *The Aspern Papers* when he met Miss Bordereau and first heard the voice heard, and loved, by Jeffrey Aspern, a feeling made even stronger an hour later when B. had returned and we were sipping sherry. Not knowing either of us, Alice was hostessing with anecdotes, most of them about Gertrude. "When T. S. Eliot said to Gertrude, 'And from whom, Miss Stein, did you learn your habit of splitting infinitives?' Gertrude said, 'I learned it from Henry James.'"

Because her hands were crippled by arthritis, Alice no longer cooked. But she loved to eat — one good meal a day, the rest coffee and an endless consumption of Pall Malls — and the three of us went to a restaurant near the rue Christine. It had banquettes along the walls, flowers on every table, and waiters who genuflected at the sight of Miss Toklas.

She was fussy about the food — "This sauce," she said, rolling it around her tongue, "has *flour* in it" — and anxious to see that B. got enough to eat. I would not hazard offering any theory about Alice B. Toklas's division of the sexes, except for one. A man, being a man, had a completely different digestive apparatus from a woman and must be stoked like a furnace.

How proud I was of B. that day, how proud I am still. His appetite was equivalent to mine, but Alice would not let him stop after the *langoustines au gratin* and the *loup sur fenouil* that sufficed for her and me. She insisted that he follow them with an entrecôte and the appropriate red wine (we had been drinking a lot of white with the fish) and said that he could not say he had dined there without sampling the *glace au vanille,* which was sprinkled with the restaurant's special praline powder. On and on he ate, dying I knew, and I loved him for his courage.

Alice liked B., as well she might. He was charming, intelligent, and devoted to her book. In the years when she could no longer see to write, he found secretaries to whom she could dictate, and the last few pages were dictated to him. What surprised me was that she appeared to like me, too. But I am not sure: Alice hid extraordinary perversity under a seemingly helpless directness. When the book was published, she wrote in B.'s copy, "To —— L ——," giving a wrong first name, "who made only one mistake and never knew what it was."

A devout Catholic, devout as only a convert can be — although Alice claimed that hers was no conversion but a return, given that the nurse of her infancy had had her baptized without her Jewish parents' knowledge — she found a certain link to holy order in my own born Catholicism. Liking clothes — her only coat was made by Balmain — she approved of mine. Very much a lady, she responded to my shyness and good manners, although she may have found me dull.

There was one day, though, during those two weeks in May when I carried my second child *in utero* around the city in which I had hoped she would be conceived, when I think Alice truly liked me. The three of us were walking down the rue Christine, which was very narrow, to Lapérouse for lunch. A car came along, and since Alice was too frail to step out of the gutter quickly, I picked her up and put her on the sidewalk. She was mortified: to be lifted like a baby, and by a woman so hugely pregnant.

"But I do this all the time," I said. "My grandmother is very fat, and the only way she can get out of her rocker is by rocking back and forth very quickly until she gains momentum. Then she launches herself forward, like a rocket. I always catch her just before she lands in my lap."

Alice closed her eyes and laughed, knowing that I was telling the truth, that I thought little of picking up eighty-year-olds. Since her fragility meant little to me, it could, for a little while anyway, mean little to her.

She was sentimental about my pregnancies. Maybe she thought I was doing what a woman *should* do, unless she was a Gertrude or a Janet Flanner, in which case other rules applied. I remember her praising Picasso's wife Jacqueline because, or so it sounded to me, she was a slave. When she heard that mutual friends were finally divorcing — Alice seemed to be the only person in Paris who did not know they had not spoken in years, or did she? — she told me of her concern for their children, then wondered aloud if anyone who dressed as badly as the wife did could have made any man happy.

When she died, she was buried in a dark Balmain suit ("Pierre has given Gertrude a black bride," Janet Flanner, or somebody like Janet Flanner, said) in Père Lachaise, to which I plan to go sometime, to put flowers on her grave. We always took Alice yellow roses, in memory of Gertrude. I will take yellow roses that day as well, in memory of her, and in memory of me. In memory of Paris, too.

Alice was not to die for nearly ten years yet, though, and now we are sitting in Chez L'Ami Louis, watching as she tips a snail shell to her mouth and drinks the garlic butter. Tomorrow B. and I will lunch at La Tour d'Argent for the very first (and my very last) time, sitting by a tall window and watching raindrops dimple the Seine. In the afternoon we will take the boat-train to Le Havre, to the United States. We have bought a case of Taittinger Blanc de Blancs, more copper pots, and a pile of *tabliers,* those little smocks French children wear, for Kate. B. reclines in the top bunk reading manuscripts and I recline in the bottom bunk rereading Evelyn Waugh, and together we are as rich as Croesus and as soigné as Gerald and Sara Murphy.

Six weeks later, on a hot July night, our second child arrives, on a sea of Richebourg because we have been at a dinner party and all that talk about alcohol in pregnancy is far in the future. She is the girl we knew she would be, and right away we name her Margaret, after my grandmother.

Margaret is very plump, has a thicket of black hair and no space between her eyebrows. "She looks," B. says, "like an Armenian innkeeper."

"She has my father's eyes," I say. Brown (eventually), turned down at the outer corners, they are the mark the Lord set on her.

44 Jane Street

· 1 ·

KATHERINE, who had just learned to drink from a cup, returned to the bottle, pulling desperately on the nipple, her eyes anxious and her fat hands gripping fiercely. But she was kind, so kind, brushing her sister's hair at bedtime and retreating quietly to her little back bedroom after we had put on her sleep cap, a felt cone that had come with her copy of *Goodnight Moon*. But first we had taken her out to the areaway to wave to the one star (I think it is Venus) that faithfully shines upon New York City. Margaret, sleepy as a dormouse, was ensconced in the bassinet beside our bed. And we had begun the hunt for the most elusive of all Manhattan spaces, a Village apartment big enough for four.

On the Upper West Side you could find big apartments — "If worse comes to worst, we can always move to the Upper West Side" was said at least once during any Village dinner party featuring new parents. But giving up Greenwich Village would have meant giving up not only its sweet, seedy streets but a certain self-image. B. and I were Villagers; we bore (I told myself) a noble heritage. Never mind that the cobwebs at Julius's bar were fake, or that the historically literary Chumley's seemed as fusty as a provincial museum. Marianne Moore had worked at the Hudson Street branch of the New York Public Library! Mary McCarthy had lived on Bank Street! And e. e. cummings still lived on Patchin Place! Once, as I was leaving a Sixth Avenue grocery, I noticed that the brown paper bags that were to be delivered to me were nestled against the brown paper bags that were to be delivered to Djuna Barnes. "You'll never guess whose order was next to ours," I said to B. when I got home. "Djuna Barnes! *Nightwood!*"

Early one morning, about to share a cab to our respective offices ("My talent is my bank account," B. would boom when I complained of the extravagance. "I can't afford to arrive frazzled"), we walked instead into a real estate agency. The agent was on the phone. "It doesn't have anything right now but space," she was saying to somebody, "but the landlord's willing to do some work on it. So let me know if you're interested."

Ten minutes later we ourselves were looking at the place that didn't have anything but space: a basement and parlor floor on Jane Street, way over west near the garbage pier.

Jane Street is in an area of docks and warehouses, a few tenements, a few big apartment buildings, and a lot of nineteenth-century houses. Some Irish still lived there then — it was the old Eighth Ward — and even though it had started to "come up," as the real estate agent put it, it was so far from the subways and so close to the meat market (where turn a corner and you were apt to run smack into a carcass dangling from a chain) that many people regarded moving there as the same as moving to hell and gone. Still do, for that matter.

Not I. When the wind blows from the west one can smell the Hudson, and the houses are low, and there are field mice in the gardens. Even now, when the old refrigeration plant and some of the old livery stables have been turned into apartments, the only nightwalkers tend to be drunks shaking their fists at fire hydrants and yelling "Motherfucker!" at the dust-obscured sky.

Dogs bark as in the country here, deep-throated roars from collies and big mongrels, and the soprano yips of Yorkies and Lhasa Apsos are only just beginning to be heard. In those days there were not even any supermarkets near Jane Street, only one newsstand, one delicatessen, and a tattered triangular park with metal swings and a sandpit. Jane Street was on the edge

— of the city, of the river, of respectability — and it was a hideout. Walking home from the subway, the houses and people dwindling as I traveled west, the trees growing fewer, the river smell coming up stronger, the traffic quieting, almost disappearing, I felt as if I were entering a stockade.

The house faced north, an ordinary red brick with a fire escape that spoiled its facade. I have no idea what the interior looks like now, but once the first two floors were beautiful. Or so we thought, and so I still think, even though the ground floor was torrid in summer and the parlor floor, with an air conditioner blasting from either end, like a meat locker.

Our landlord was a small, skinny Irishman with five children (a year or two later they were six) and a small, trim wife on whom he doted. His grandparents and their parents had worked the docks and run the livery stables, and it was from them that he had inherited the house. "The minute anybody around here got any money," he told us, "they put down parquet floors. On Saturday nights you'd get a trio — a sax, maybe, and a drummer, and if you had a piano, a guy to play it — and there'd be dancing in the living room. Now the Italians . . . they liked to put down linoleum." The Village was to him what Bristol was to me: a place where the streets were as thronged with the dead as with the living.

Matty — his name was Matty — had had to gut the top two floors of the house to make bedrooms for his kids, most of whom were at parochial school. But our two floors he could return to what they had once been, balking only at ripping up the parquet to expose what I was convinced would be pumpkin pine floorboards beneath.

He installed a new kitchen sink, out of which rats ran until the plumber discovered an unplugged hole that led to a tortuous tunnel that led to the sewer system. He had some of the stones in the little drying yard raised so we could plant a garden and replaced the sagging board fence with wooden palings. He cut off a corner of the parlor floor linen closet and put in a small second bathroom, and he had the old shutters prised from their niches in the dining room and our bedroom.

And we? We were giddy with wallpaper, which we put in the hall and the children's room and the tiny guest room. We installed stair carpeting, a washing machine that emptied into the downstairs tub, and a dryer that was vented out the bathroom window. B. and a friend of his worked night after night building bookcases, then gave up and let a carpenter take over. "Please, Matty," we begged, "can we have a new refrigerator?" He smiled and gave us $150 toward a fourteen-cubic-footer from Sears. Oh my! Let me walk through that house again. It makes me happy to walk through that house.

The dining room was on the ground-floor front, but it was not really a dining room yet, because we did not have a table. We visualized something oval, something mahogany, something, we said, "like an Irish hunt table." Not that we had ever seen an Irish hunt table, you understand, or had the foggiest notion of how to go about finding one. But we loved the term "Irish hunt table." We loved it like we loved "Georgian silver" and "Chinese export porcelain." Own them, we thought, and you are armored for life.

The walls were cream, and on three of them were floor-to-ceiling bookcases, packed with books left over from college, books we had bought at the secondhand stores on Fourth Avenue, books sent to B. by friends in publishing, and what B. called "the New Yorker collection," which is to say the collected works of Liebling, White, McNulty, and Mitchell, all of whom we idolized. The slate fireplace on the west wall didn't work, so we put an old metal milk-bottle basket sprayed yellow on the hearth and stuffed it with dried flowers. The slant-top desk and Windsor chair were in a corner by the window, and an outsize blue wing chair lighted by one of the standing lamps from West Eleventh Street was by the door.

The big square kitchen had a brick fireplace that didn't work, either, an old Chambers stove (no more Royal Rose for me!), enameled cabinets brought from Perry Street, a round deal table and rush-seated chairs, a high chair and a playpen. In that roomy kitchen, I told myself when I first saw it, I would put up jellies. I would attempt croissants. I would finally make the veau Prince Orloff, from *Mastering the Art of French Cooking, Volume One,* that I and all my fellow cooks aspired to.

The living room, on the parlor floor, was a measure of how far we had come. The wing chair, couch, and loveseat traveled with us from Perry Street, but now we had a Portuguese needlepoint rug and a mahogany sideboard (eighteenth century, English) and a round, cloth-covered table centered by a lamp from Bloomingdale's that had cost $75. There were many more pictures and, eventually, tucked in a drawer in the sideboard, a pen-and-ink by Andrew Wyeth (gift of the artist), a Cruikshank sketchbook (gift to me from my husband), and a caricature by Max Beerbohm (gift to my husband from a friend). The living room also had, as did the bedroom, dentil moldings and a slate fireplace that worked.

The living room opened onto the bedroom, which was actually the front parlor, and although they could be closed off from each other by huge sliding doors, they seldom were, because we liked the long view into that serene white room. Also, we liked to show it off.

Like all my bedrooms, this one was impossibly virginal, suitable for a nun with a passion for pillows. The walls, curtains, bedspread, the flokati rug, even the flowers in the ironstone pitcher on the fireplace mantel were white. A wing chair and the chaise longue were blue and white toile. The three-quarter bed had been replaced at last, by a brand-new Bloomingdale's queen-size with an artfully rustic Spanish headboard, also Bloomingdale's. The quasi-mahogany sideboard had gone to the dump, and now we had an early eighteenth-century

American pine blanket chest. All that remained of Twenty-first Street, but for a few glasses, prints, and odds and ends of china, was the quasi-mahogany bureau.

With a fire in the fireplace, B. on the chaise longue with one book, and me in bed with another, we could imagine we were in the ultimate country inn, the inn that, in the autumn I was pregnant with Katherine, we had looked for all over Vermont. Here it was, just like the bluebird of happiness, right in our own back yard.

Meanwhile, as we read, two little girls slept as if couched on zephyrs on the south side of the parlor floor, in a room that had bunny wallpaper, a nightlight that looked like a Staffordshire cottage, and a bookcase crammed with the collected Beatrix Potter. Snow White was in a youth bed and Rose Red was in a crib, and next to them was the little blue and white guest room that one of them would have one day.

Because I recognize emotions only in retrospect, I didn't know that I was happy. As always, there was something nagging at my mind's corners. But I did know that I had all that it is proper in this world to wish for.

Soon after she was born, and just before we moved to 44 Jane Street, our little one, our Margaret, got funny patches on her face. Her hair started falling out in huge clumps, with bits of her scalp attached, and we became afraid to comb or brush it. Her eyes shrank to slits, and stuff oozed from under the lids and out her ears. There were cracks at the creases in her elbows and behind her knees, out of which the same stuff oozed. Eventually the cracks widened and began to bleed. The pediatrician said she had eczema and sent us to a dermatologist. When he saw her, tears sprouted in his eyes and scared us into speechlessness. "This is bad," he answered to our unasked question. "She can't retain skin."

The dermatologist sent us to an allergist, who said infant

eczema was inherited, and did either of us come from families with a history of eczema or asthma? My husband said he did. I called his mother. Oh yes, she said, B. had had asthma as a child, and his nephews had had eczema. I had married a killer.

My mother had said that I had a nasty tongue, that some-day I would call my husband a dirty Jew. The words were not in my head until she put them there, and I had spent so much of my life keeping my mouth shut that I didn't know what kind of tongue I had, if any. But now I feared that this dreadful mouth of mine would open and devils would leap out. So I clamped my lips, and "If I had known about those allergies I never would have married you" was written all over my face. My husband was silent, too, because he was ashamed and guilty, and because there was no way to expiate original sin. Between us lay our baby, who we thought was dying, and words that, unspoken, were as loud as cymbals clashing.

I kept the hood up on Margaret's carriage, even in the supermarket, so strangers could not see her clearly. If they did, they asked what was the matter, should she be wearing a bonnet, was she getting enough sun?

A second doctor, the head of a hospital's allergy depart-ment, kept losing Margaret's records and confusing her with her other patients. She said she wanted to take blood from Margaret, reduce it to a serum, inject it into a paid, allergy-free donor, and test the donor for the baby's allergies. "You mustn't let her do it," said a mat-mate (I never knew her name) at Kounovsky's Gym, where, in leotard and tights, I tumbled, trapezed, and swung on the rings twice a week. "The blood loss is terrible."

"Rosehip tea and beef broth cure everything," an ex-ballet dancer said, making me hate her for her mindlessness.

"My son used to look like that," the old Italian contractor who was painting 44 Jane Street said.

"How was he treated?" I asked.

"He died."

In the office — I had gone back to work when Margaret was four weeks old — I could lose myself in work. I have always been able to lose myself in work. But if someone asked me how the baby was coming along, I grew nervous, desperate to leave my desk and go home. *She won't die,* I told myself, *if I keep my eyes on her. If I close them for a second, though, she'll slip away.* (Years later, the old maternal griefs having returned, I stayed up all night with a sick kitten, believing that keeping my eyes on it as I had on Margaret was a way of pinning it to life.)

In the evening B. and I sat in the living room, Margaret sleeping on my lap, in a silence thick as heavy dust. How could we have spoken? All we had to talk about was his guilt and my rage. When we met he used to tell me how he felt, but he had stopped, because although I listened, I could not absorb. I, however, had rarely spoken of how I felt about anything. I did not want him to know, let alone anyone else to know, afraid that if I plunged into my head, I would come up with a forkful of worms. So we sat silent, Dr. Franklin once again dispensed with, Jerry moved away, and neither of us able to leap over the wall to the other.

At last we found the right doctor, the one who knew how to care for our baby. "She's allergic to *everything*," he said, "so right now I'd rather treat the symptoms than the source." Margaret, slathered with cortisone cream, sluiced with tar baths, switched from my breast to soybean milk, grew curly black hair and cheeks like pink peonies. Once, when her doctor was lecturing to the class he taught at University Hospital, he used Margaret as his subject, pointing to her as she sat, fat, naked, and happy, on a table in the classroom. I stood in the corner beaming, as proud as if she had just won a contest for Most Beautiful Baby.

But as the eczema disappeared, asthma surfaced, and sometimes at night we heard her breathing turn to rales. Then B. would sit for hours in the bathroom, Margaret on his lap, the shower pounding and the room steaming and his eyes a misery. Meanwhile I pretended sleep and turned my back when, the baby no longer wheezing and back in her crib, I felt him sliding into bed.

It was too much. When the baroness, soon to leave *Mademoiselle* and devote herself to biography and opinionated gardening, asked me if I would consider working full-time, I said yes on the spot. I was flattered, of course, and proud to be earning my own money. But the real reason I leaped was that those months of standing over Margaret, watching and crying, had convinced me that I was not fit to deal with crises. Hoppy had returned, Hoppy who had slung Kate over her shoulder like a dishtowel and sung and whistled her into sleep, and my children would be safer with her than with me. But I am telling only half the truth. Maybe only a quarter of it. The rest of the truth is that I was unable to bear loving my children so much. Loving left me weak, skinless. Ideally I would have liked Katherine and Margaret sewn to my armpits, secured to me. Or, better yet, kicking and turning in my stomach, where I could keep them safe forever. I had to be away from my daughters because loving them was making me crazy.

B.'s being around — if together we had sat between the youth bed and the crib, as I did every night alone, singing "Rock-a-Bye, Baby" — might have eased my obsessiveness. But he had been offered a job in Boston a few months before Margaret was born. "See if they'll let you be there part-time," I said, and consigned him to a room in some club or other. I was not about to move anywhere, but especially not to Boston, which was too close to the permanent three-o'clock-in-the-afternoon that I imagined a life in Bristol would have been. Besides, I loved my job, not because it was engrossing — although it was usually amusing — but because it was all mine.

So he was gone from Tuesday at dawn through Thursday at sunset, and when he came home on Thursday nights I was rattled, resentful of an intruder into my beautiful circle of work and children. By the weekend I was glad he was in the house; I'd gotten used to him again. But when Tuesday arrived he was gone once more, and then I would reenter the magic place, all females, two of them babies, and all of them smelling sweet.

"Mary," a friend asked, "aren't you nervous? Didn't you see *Captain's Paradise?*"

I laughed, not yet having acquired imagination. My husband and my father were the only men I had ever known well, and Papa was faithless only in dying. Since B. had taken over where Papa left off, he would be no different. He was not the same man, I knew that. And yet, in a way, he was.

I do not know now how I discovered that I should have been nervous. All I remember is a civilized conversation in the living room, my hand shaking whenever I lifted a cigarette to my mouth and B.'s eyes opaque behind a pipe which kept going out. "How could a woman with children," I am asking him, "do that to another woman with children?" What had I ever done to deserve such treatment from a perfect stranger?

I absolved him, poor man alone in Boston because his wife refused to move. But not her, not that traitor to her own gender. Nor me, the wife who hadn't packed up her children and chattels and left town with her husband. And if I had? Best not to think of the boredom and, I suspect, the drinking that would have ensued. But something my father had often said when my sister and I left for parties and proms started sounding in my ears again. "Always come home with the man what brung ya," he had charged, and I had disobeyed.

Margaret got well, Katie got beautiful, the girlfriend was discarded — how and when I never knew, being too courteous to ask — and Boston dissolved into the past. It was no place for someone as fast-paced as B. or, for that matter, for a Jew. When his boss heard that I had come from coastal Rhode Island, he said, "Oh! She's maritime." That was his way of saying, "She's okay." B., I knew, because a childhood spent next to New England's old money had thinned my skin almost to transparency, would never be okay.

No, B. was better off in New York, which is infinitely capacious, and better off as a literary agent wheeling and dealing and caviling and cajoling and doing it all with seamless charm. One of his colleagues called him "the Master."

Deep into the evening, flopped on the chaise longue, he took call after call from writers who depended on their agents like patients do on their psychiatrists. Their wives, too. Writers' husbands I knew little about — there seemed so few of them — but they struck me as docile. Writers' wives were not. They were martyrs to literature, all of them, and God forbid you shouldn't know it.

One night the ultimate martyr phoned. During an argument her husband had chased her through the room with a hammer or a chain or an axe or some other piece of heavy equipment. Somehow she had diverted him out the front door and locked it, and he was now circling the house, weapon in hand, feet occasionally entangled in pachysandra. Calling the police never entered her mind. Instead she called his agent, who lived one thousand miles away. "This," I barked, "is the limit!"

The husband was coaxed inside, weaponless, with the promise that his agent, the Great Healer, was on the phone, and B. lured him to tranquillity with his Thorazine voice. I, distracted from my book, my beautiful bedroom, my beautiful life, said I was sorry the writer and his wife hadn't shot it out, thus leaving us in peace.

In truth, this particular writer's wife was one of the few I really liked. I liked her because she was frightened, because she always expected the marriage to slip out from under her, because she knew about the abyss. Other wives, most wives, I disliked. They had, it seemed to me, certain tools I would never possess, the marital equivalent of street smarts. They could wheedle, they could pounce, they could own. I, who would have made some lucky woman a fine husband, didn't know how to do any of those things. My father's daughter, I had been a gentleman all my life.

I was afraid of wives — I saw them as smug, smooth-feathered hens — and the wives I feared most were astronauts' wives. There they were in *Life* magazine, with names like Joan and Annie: stalwart and true, and the first ones to be phoned after their hubbies had spoken to the president. Why do I think they all had sons named Chip? What was their secret? What did they know? What was the sorority grip, and why was I never taught it?

B., gregarious as well as deeply involved in his work, stayed out late at dinners and at parties. I, being neither, stayed home with the babies and the books. My husband, overworked and high-strung, would vomit late at night. I, who tend to conduct my illnesses as do dying dogs — sitting alone, staring into corners — did not realize that grownups as well as children need to have their heads held as they bend over the toilet bowl, and left him to his retching.

Work exhausted me, too, but not intellectually. How could it? I was, after all, sitting at a desk writing "Pink brocade, its skirt plumped with layers of petticoats." But it was difficult for me to talk to too many people for too long, or to listen to the endless nattering on the Graybar Building's elevators. What I wanted from marriage, apart from the children and the pleasure of knowing that I was not out there on the street alone, with the wind lifting my skirt and the mud speckling the backs of my legs, was a clean, well-lighted tomb in which I could spend the evening restoring myself for the next day. I was tired, too. When at last I finally drifted into sleep, I could feel the bed falling into the center of the earth.

· 2 ·

EVERY JANUARY, B.T.B. went to Paris for the collections, installing herself in a suite in the Plaza Athénée and hiding her liquor on a ledge inside the living room fireplace. "Why tempt the help?" she used to say. Then, companioned by *Mademoiselle*'s Paris editor, a taut, thin Frenchwoman who was aunt to Leslie Caron, she did Dior and Chanel and everybody else worth covering that season. Mrs. B. had been going to Paris for years — her first trip was on the *Berengaria* — and although she never learned to speak French, she loved the tag lines. *"Merci millefois,"* she would say in thanks, *"A bientot"* in leaving.

In July the head of the fashion department made the same trip. Both sent sketches, by a man named MoMo, and notes for copy and captions back by overnight flight to New York. We — the art director and two copywriters — then worked all the next night to squeeze them into the next issue. The result, four pages of undistinguished drawings and telegraphese, was invariably ugly. But not to B.T.B. and the rest of the fashion department. *Mademoiselle,* like *Vogue* and *Bazaar,* had reported Paris!

Our second winter at 44 Jane Street, I suggested an article that would track a young designer for the two weeks leading up to his first show. The baroness's replacement, a middle-aged woman with famous friends, who always put on lipstick before answering the phone if told the caller was a man, liked the idea. "Now let me see," she mused. "Who do I know who's in Paris right now?"

"But *I* want to do it," I said, surprising myself as much as I surprised her. Never before had I said "I want" about anything that had to do with work. "Yours," a friend had pontificated, "is a passive personality."

I had been afraid to fly — "Which one of us is going to be on the ill-fated plane?" B. would ask about the tortuous travel plans that would assure that our children did not lose both parents in a crash — and afraid to write, and now both fears had evaporated in the face of that furious "I want."

The night before the flight, I lay in bed beside my husband as frightened as if it had been execution eve. I do not understand why I thought I was taking an irreversible step. I had no goal beyond writing that one article, no ideas for others, and little interest in advancing what I would have been embarrassed to call a career. The term was pretentious, even low-class — the kind of word used by the kind of people who called a college economics class "econ" rather than the Ivy League–preferred "eck." So when I cried and apologized to B. for leaving him, and said over and over again that I was sorry I had to go, I can only assume it was because my gut was telling me something about myself that my head was not ready to hear.

B. was proud of his wife: at last she was living up to her potential. I must not forget to call on Alice, must not forget some tinned truffles at Fauchon, must not forget his sandalwood soap. He had written to so-and-so, so there was at least one good dinner on tap; and surely so-and-so would be free for lunch one day; and no, I must not worry that people would not like me, because of course they would. I left the next morning, blessed with my husband's good will and competent child care and possessed by a sadness that has grayed a portion of every day I have lived since. Why did I have to make that trip, when all I had ever wanted (or so I still tell myself) was to be a good wife and a perfect mother and to sleep in peace?

My room was on the Left Bank, on the top floor of the Hôtel Pont-Royal, and its ceiling slanted like a garret's. It was small, too, just big enough for me and a typewriter and a tiny portable radio, which I stuck in a wooden bureau drawer so the sound would be better. Because it was January I had packed warm flannel nightgowns, and laughed every night on seeing that the chambermaid who turned down the bed and laid a nightgown athwart its pillows invariably pinched in its waist. Sexy granny gowns! Too funny! "You brought flannel night-gowns to *Paris*, Mary?" B.T.B., who arrived a week later, said. "Suppose something unexpected should arise?"

I was flattered that B.T.B. thought me capable of racy conduct, thereby admitting me to the company of the dashing, but the idea of sharing my bed was incredible. There was no one in the world, no movie star even, for whom I would have sacrificed the pleasure of sleeping alone in that room with its view over the rooftops and its scent of disinfectant and Gau-loises and Jolie Madame.

I had never been alone before, unless not having a room-mate in college counts, and I kept discovering new things about myself. The pleasure of my own company, for one, and the curiosity that sent me bravely out into the streets with bad French and no sense of direction. But I never got lost, not once, and I began to acquire a trust, still with me, in my feet's wisdom. My body was becoming my house. I ambulated as securely as a turtle.

And I was happy, so happy I was afraid to acknowledge the feeling lest, once named, it would fly away. Sitting one noon in a restaurant near the Madeleine with my omelet and my packet of Disque Bleus, wearing my fun fur and my Pucci dress and my I. Miller shoes, I said to myself, "Now you've got everything Papa and B. ever wanted for you."

So what if I had run my entire life on my husband's and

father's engines? Who is to say that my own engine, assuming it ever existed or was distinguishable from theirs, would have been preferable? Not I.

Some evenings I spent in my room, bent over a bowl of soup, my notes, and the phone. The article had to be finished before I left Paris, and since the only criticism I trusted or would abide by was B.'s, I spent a fortune calling New York and reading him the day's work. If he said it was okay, it was. Anyone else's opinion was unimportant. The reading over, we would chat about the children and what he was doing and what the weather was in New York (it was gray and rainy in Paris), and then I would do something I had not done since we were in college and he had called me every night on the dorm phone. "You hang up first," I would say. "No, you hang up first," he would say, and then, unwilling to be the first to cut the connection, we would arrange to put our receivers back in their cradles at precisely the same time.

In college, once I had hung up the phone, I would feel as though I had lost an arm. But not now. Now I felt whole again, because of the bliss of returning to a silence broken only by the typewriter's hesitant staccato and an occasional *whoop-whoop-whoop* from a passing police car. I was concentrating at last, and all my bits and pieces were coalescing into one self-sufficient self.

Other evenings I dined with B.'s friends, or with new friends I had met while following the couturier around. They liked me, they asked me out again and again, they thought I was amusing. Maybe I was, but mostly I was a new face, a new audience for the old act. No matter. I was working without a net — my husband — and I was not falling down.

There was one man, Philippe (I cannot even remember his last name, and in any case it was never important), a few years younger than I, who took me dancing. He wore Cardin suits and came from Provence, was small-boned, elegant, and faintly reminiscent of Colette's Chéri. More than that I cannot say, because I knew no more of him than that, only what my imagination made of him. It turned him into France, and Paris, my Paris, in particular.

In Paris it was the month of the Beatles. They were performing at the Olympia and were reliably reported to have just left every discothèque one had just entered. "The Beatles were here only a minute ago," I heard in every dim, smoky room. "You just missed them."

I can't remember ever smoking or drinking in any of those discos, only dancing and looking back at my little round table to see if my quilted Chanel bag was still there. Actually, every little round table bore a quilted Chanel bag. They were membership cards.

The big word was *"yé-yé,"* used to describe everything from the cut of a skirt to the curve of a curl, and the big song was "Et Maintenant." When that was played, conversation halted, hips ground together, partner eyeballed partner, and the sound of heavy breathing swamped the room. When Philippe and I danced, my groin hurt, and although we kept a proper inch or two apart, I confused the thought with the deed and deemed myself an adulteress.

Toward dawn he would drive wildly through the empty Paris streets. Or maybe he was not really driving wildly. Maybe it was only the smallness of his car and the screech it made when he took corners that made me think we were speeding, heading for a crash, careless of our lives. One evening he stopped in front of Notre-Dame, which, the illumination gone, had returned to medieval darkness.

"This makes me think of François Villon," I said, "and the wolves that stalked the walls of Paris."

"Vous êtes formidable," he breathed, and took my hand.

I cried. I was not *formidable.* I was simply the virgin

mother of two experiencing the late adolescence she had never
had, too naive to recognize the melt in the stomach, the sense
of shiver, as the sensations of the twenty-year-old she had
never been.

On the afternoon I left Paris, Philippe took me to the
airport and stayed on the observation desk waving until takeoff.
I cried again, cried all the way home. I was on Air France,
stretched out on three seats, and an old babushkaed Polish
woman across the aisle kept looking over at me, sighing and
clucking and nodding and wanting to help. But she had no
English, and the babushka and her anxious monkey eyes and
baggy coat and fat, spread feet only made me cry the harder.

B., the children, and Hoppy were at the airport. Margaret,
sitting on my lap, wet my skirt on the cab ride into the city. She
was eighteen months old, and too hearty even for double diapers
and rubber pants. Katie's hair ribbon was flying and Hoppy was
chatting and my husband was silent. He knew me, much better than I knew myself, and he saw my pink eyes and the way
they dodged his.

I am not much given to playing "If I had" or "If I hadn't,"
much preferring to stay with "It would have happened anyway."
But that last is usually a lie, and I am not one to kid myself. I
am sorry I went to Paris, because when I returned I was full of
myself and starved for more of me. Or am I sorry? I do not
know. I am mixed up. But I do know that there have been many
years when I wished I could have walked into that little group
at the airport, never to emerge again. I see them — the husband who looked like Montgomery Clift in his Harrods' raincoat, the nurse in her white uniform, the little girl dancing in
her hair ribbons, and the baby bulwarked in her diapers — and
they haunt me, still there, still waiting at Kennedy.

My mother had said I was born an old maid. My husband had
told me I would make a wonderful widow. Always eager to

accept others' definitions of myself — they saved me the boredom, and the pain, of having to make my own — I argued with
both, that being my way, and silently agreed with both, that
also being my way. But now I had to think, and I could only do
that if I was alone. So I made what seemed to me a perfectly
logical request: I asked B. to move out for a few weeks.

So B. moved to a friend's apartment down the street, more
dwindled by my request than I had been by his adultery. Which
does not imply that I was the larger character, only that he was,
for a while anyway, the more human. And I lived for a month
the life that a few years later became the only one I knew.

In bed at night, the children asleep, I had long talks with
me. So satisfying! I said, *Papa would not have wanted me to
have mourned him for so many years.* So I buried him. I thought
about Philippe. Who was he, anyway? A figment of my imagination, really. So I buried him. I thought about B. Who was he?
The only man I had ever wanted to marry. My father's surro-
gate. My floor. My door to the world. So I asked him to come
home.

He came home, and he cried. But I did not know it then. He
cried because the relief of being away from me had eclipsed
the hurt of being asked to go. He had met someone, or, more
likely, someone had been served up to him — when a formerly
unavailable man is suddenly made free, all the world turns
Pandarus — and he had had fun. He had had a good time. But
I am guessing. I do not know what his life was without me, but
I think it was like being on parole.

A few months later, in December, we gave a party to cele-
brate our eleventh wedding anniversary. "For this I'm coming
wrapped in the Israeli flag," Leo Lerman said. "I never thought
you'd make it."

Neither did I, and I was tremendously pleased with myself, with my husband, and with the exceptional sanity and
staying power that had put us beyond anything so weak-

minded as divorce. One could defeat anything, death only excluded, if one just put one's *mind* to it. Not enough people put their *minds* to things.

I had spent the previous evening making pâtés and dips, deviling eggs, stuffing mushrooms, and baking a ham. We had hired a bartender, but everything else was done by me. My grandmother's contemptuous "store-bought" had left me with the style of a house-proud nineteenth-century New England housewife.

My office assistant said our friends were absolutely glamorous. Our apartment was jammed with writers and editors and agents and their pretty, thirtyish wives. No one was divorced or dying yet — that started a few years later — and our children, in their best dresses and hair ribbons, were made much of. Almost everyone there had children, too, all of them about to be launched toward New York's private schools.

No one had bad breath; no one was overweight but for one literary agent, who was discovered in the kitchen picking at the hambone. But since her weight served as a metaphor for her arrogant charm, her two hundred plus pounds were considered okay. No one got drunk, since half the guests were drinking dry vermouth on the rocks with a twist of lemon. Several of the writers were stars of the month, just about the right number, because too many of them and everyone would be wondering if he was standing in the right orbit, only one of them and you got awed and silent guests.

The hostess has had her hair done in a kind of Jackie Kennedy bouffant at the Tempo Beauty Salon on West Twelfth Street (stingy, practical, she will never drop a cent at Kenneth's), and is elegant in a long gray Donald Brooks cut low over breasts so small (though sweet) that she looks dressed even when she is naked. She is balancing a glass of dry vermouth and a cigarette, keeping an eye on the children, count-

ing the stuffed mushrooms, and greeting all and sundry. She is
a wonder. She has crested.

Casting yourself in character parts is a pleasant way to trundle
through life. It promises continuity. Those were the years, I say
now, when I was a young matron, thus implying that there
were other years when I was a this, other years when I was a
that, years to come when I will be something else entirely.
Young matron. Yes, I was certainly that.

Early in the morning I walked Kate and Mag down Hudson Street to their little Episcopal school. Like all our crowd,
we had abjured the public schools. They were all, except for
the legendary P.S. 6 on the Upper East Side, for which parents
fought and killed, "impossible."

Rose Red hung on to my right hand, Snow White hung on
to my left, until they broke free and ran through the gate and
into the little playground. The school was banked by a very old
church and early nineteenth-century brick houses — Bret Harte
had lived in one of them — and in my memory yellow leaves
are forever scudding along the sidewalk and the air is forever
crisp and blue.

Next I would step off the curb, hail a cab, and pick up B.,
who was waiting, attaché case in hand, on the corner of Jane
Street. He would drop me off on Park, next to the alleyway that
led to the back of the Graybar Building, with the incantatory
"Good luck, I love you" I insisted on before I could start work.
Then I would enter the office I shared with two assistants, to
laugh a lot and write copy between spurts of gossip.

Two nights a week I stopped at the Tempo Beauty Salon
for a shampoo and set. The Tempo was cheap. Even better, it
was reminiscent of the place my mother went to in Bristol for
her permanents and manicures, but where hers had a radio on
the windowsill, this one had a television set on the counter. I

saw that Vietnamese colonel, I think he was, blow a hole through a captive's head on that television set. Then I walked home, to Snow White and Rose Red, who were gobbling down fried whiting and collard greens. Hoppy had retired. Our new housekeeper was from North Carolina, and I was running, although I didn't know it and had not even heard the term, the greatest soul food kitchen in New York.

We entertained quite often, and if I did not shine in conversation, I did not care. B. was the shine; I was glad to be the chamois. Feeding people was what pleased me. I thought myself a goddess when my hands were in dough or skinning a chicken or hulling strawberries.

We were invited to many parties, too, but I skipped most of them, and the only evening that sticks in my mind was a New Year's Eve in the dark, crowded apartment of a literary agent who chain-smoked cigarettes clamped in a roach holder on her index finger. "There we were," I told my assistants the next workday, "like the audience at a bullfight. The wives were sitting around the ring, and the matadors, the husbands, were strutting in the center. The only woman who got out there with them was Elaine Dundy, but of course *she'd* had a bestseller."

No, there's another evening that also sticks in my mind. We were dining, on the Upper West Side, with a man who had been famous because of his talent and was famous now mostly because of his eight wives. The eighth was there, a former movie actress whose eyes swam in their sockets like guppies in a bowl and who kept repeating, her fist pounding her palm, that her husband was *a real man.*

He, balding, was on the other side of the room talking about Spinoza, about whom he could quote reams of other people's opinions. You could not beat him in debate. Disagree with one of his assessments, which were never his to begin with, and he would hit you with Kierkegaard, say, quoted *in toto.*

Later, in the cab, I told B. that if I had ever been mad enough to marry that man, I would still be his first and only wife. "I can't see that divorce solves anything."

"I know you can't," he said, and kept silence all the way home.

The silences are what I remember, not conversations, not even arguments. But then, we never did argue, not really. We had too much in common.

We read a lot, for instance, and we were as one when it came to our children's educations. We were accomplished eaters, drank only grape derivatives, and enjoyed driving through Europe. We even looked a bit alike. "If we were meeting for the first time," I said the day before he left, "you'd like me."

Perhaps it was, in the end, a matter of style, not content. Myself, holding Kate's hand, emerging on Easter Sunday from a church he hated as only a man whose cousin, the Lochinvar of his childhood, had died in the Lincoln Brigade could hate it. Myself, bustling in from a Sunday afternoon movie in which quantities of cognac had been consumed, pouring myself a stiff two fingers in emulation of the heroine and describing the film in the breathlessly chatty manner I had osmosed in assorted country clubs (no Jews allowed, Catholics, provided they looked and talked like me, only bearable) and Connecticut College. Myself, enthusing about a gymnastics class and demonstrating a headstand to a man whose last participatory athletic event had been a softball game when he was twenty-three. Myself, anxious to get sex over with so I could get to sleep. Myself, desperate with migraine and nursing an ulcer and smilin' through. Myself, talking, talking, talking to reach someone who was receding, irretrievably, into the distance. Suddenly there was so much of myself, so much to choose from, and none of it wanted.

· 3 ·

THE MANAGING EDITOR, the one with all the famous friends, resigned. She was going to *Seventeen,* where the increase in salary would more than make up for no longer being able to publish such unlikely contributers to *Mademoiselle* as Cabot Lodge and Alistair Cooke, and the personnel department — mysterious women stuffed with more secrets than the Sphinx — was shipping candidate after candidate to B.T.B.'s boudoir. All we ever saw of them was a coat, usually expensive, folded over a chair beside B.T.B.'s secretary's desk, but that was enough to set the office, Leo Lerman in particular, to trembling. We liked *Mademoiselle* just the way it was.

Leo's kingdom was a shoebox of a room crammed with a filing cabinet that might have come out of *Front Page,* an old glass-fronted bookcase, an ancient typewriter, and a big desk spilling over with papers, photographs, pens, pencils, and once, in a drawer, a family of mice. I had never known him to like any of *Mlle.*'s managing editors — they either threatened his pages or cramped his style, or both — so he was pleased when I suggested myself for the job. It was about then, I think, that he, who lived and breathed every English novel that ever was, started calling me "our Mary."

There was a certain amateurishness, a beguiling raffishness to *Mademoiselle.* One of the fashion editors was hanging out at Tim Leary's place in Millbrook, forever racing out the back door as the police were racing in the front; another, fresh from California, had framed her bulletin board with lollipops and wore skirts so short the world gasped when she bent over. B. claimed that if he was standing around the Graybar Building's lobby, he could always identify the *Mademoiselle* girls by the way they dressed ("oddly," he said) and by "something funny about their knees."

So if I felt a bit timid about going to the gym teacher who still ruled the personnel department and telling her I would like to be the next managing editor, I was not the least timid about thinking I could handle the job. *Mademoiselle* was the kind of place where you could make things up as you went along, not because anybody was ever thinking seriously about innovation or would even dream of using the word but because most of the staff was imbued with the spirit of a Mickey Rooney/Judy Garland musical. We were forever planning a show in the back yard.

Magisterial behind her bosom and her desk, the gym teacher pondered. Could I, she wondered aloud, "handle" B.T.B.? I was younger than my predecessors, had two small children, and could not be counted on to stay an hour or so after the staff went home, chatting in her office and sharing a nip or two of vodka.

"Oh, yes," I said, and got the job.

In truth, I never had to "handle" B.T.B. We got along because she was always loyal to her editors in public, even if she disagreed with them in private, and because I was not remotely duplicitous. Sometimes, though, I think I puzzled her, being perhaps the only Irish Catholic she had ever known who was neither the cook's daughter nor the child of a family like the Kennedys or the McDonnells. "But of course, the Irish *ruined* Southampton," I had once overheard her say to the managing editor with the famous friends. The latter, born in Boston and raised among the pink-cheeked and high-nosed, shared the sentiment.

Not being able to place me forced B.T.B. to put me on something like par; and besides, her snobberies were essentially innocent. "Did you know her mother was a *trained nurse?*" she once asked about an editor who, eager to ingratiate herself with a woman whose son had belonged to the Knickerbocker Grays, was overfond of mentioning her own membership in the Junior League. Trained nurses, I knew from childhood eavesdropping, had seen men who were not their husbands (assuming they had any) *naked,* and knew more than they should about birth control.

"Take me to the Plaza!" I said to B. when I phoned to tell him that I was the new managing editor. The Plaza was in honor of Fitzgerald, just as the Ritz was in honor of Hemingway. "Take me to the Ritz Bar!" I had said on the day six years before when I arrived on the boat-train from Le Havre, seven months pregnant and glowing like a lamp. I had two martinis and stole an ashtray, and B. caught my every word and tossed it into the air. Now, though, he smiled and said the right things, whatever they were, but my words never reached their target, not really. Instead they simply dropped into space.

If it wasn't like the day at the Ritz, neither was it like the last time I had been in the Plaza. That had been a few years before, when Leo Lerman and Roger Schoening, who was the art director, and I sneaked out of the office late one afternoon to see *The Leather Boys.* Suddenly the screen went blank and the little lights at the end of the aisles died and we went out onto Fifty-seventh Street, where people were scurrying like ants just dislodged from an anthill. The sky was a chill November gray, still light enough for us to see clearly, and all that told us that something was very wrong were the darkened windows of Tiffany's and Bergdorf's and Van Cleef. "Let us go to the Plaza," Leo said grandly. "They will know what is happening."

Roger and I followed him — it was like following stately, plump Buck Mulligan — into the Palm Court, where the waiters were bringing candles and the little orchestra was sawing away at Viennese waltzes. "The last night on the *Titanic,*" Leo said, delighted, and waved us to a table, where we sat for hours, Roger and I drinking whatever the waiters came up with and Leo abstemious as usual, in what we learned later was the great blackout of 1965.

The phones were not out yet, so after a long wait in a line downstairs I managed to call home and tell B. that I was not only not stuck in an elevator but ensconced in the Palm Court. Then there was nothing to do but enjoy the shadows and the candles and the Blue Danube waltz.

Once we realized that the electric power was not going to come back anytime soon, Leo started the long walk home, fifty or so blocks to his house, a raddled old beauty way up on Lexington Avenue. Along the way, he informed us later, he helped direct traffic. We were stunned.

Roger and I walked him as far as Fifth Avenue, then waited at what we assumed was a bus stop because of all the people clustered there. When a bus came, perhaps an hour later, it was as crowded as a Mexican jitney. The mood was Mexican, too. Or rather, what I imagined a Mexican mood to be. We were cheerful, we were happy, we all but danced in place.

Once in the Village, we walked west through a city that was close to invisible. I do not remember stars (although I have been told there was a full moon), or people, or sound, only Roger falling over a fire hydrant in front of the Greenwich Theater. He left me on Jane Street, then limped to his place on Greenwich Street, and I walked into a house that smelled of the chicken Hoppy had roasted in the gas oven. Her daughter was there — B. had fished her out of a nearby subway station — and was to sleep on the living room couch. Hoppy was taking the little bedroom next to the children's. A smile split B.'s face when I came in the door, and the children, bathed and in their bathrobes, capered around my knees. There we all were, safe under one roof, and there was nothing the darkness could do to any of us.

*   *   *

"Well, what do you think I ought to do first?" My new secretary, who has just arrived from *Vogue,* where mostly she answered the sportswear editor's phone, is standing in the doorway. "Maybe I should go through the files."

"That sounds like a good idea."

She laughs. I laugh. At lunch I tell a chum from the copy department that I just love my new secretary's face. "No wonder," the chum says. "She looks just like you." Back from lunch, I stare at this girl who has buried herself in the file drawers and is turning them upside down. She could be my niece, or a much younger sister. This resemblance, I figure, is a good omen.

Everyone in the office is forever looking for omens, good or bad. We read the horoscope column in *Elle;* several of us, including myself, toss the I Ching every morning; and one of us is studying numerology. Nobody takes any of this seriously, but we love having a couple of tools with which to grasp life's vagaries. That B.T.B. and I are so unexpectedly harmonious, for instance, is laid by the office seers to our both being Tauruses.

When I tell B. that evening of what my secretary had found in the file drawers — manuscripts going back through two of my predecessors, often accompanied by angry letters from their authors demanding to know when they would run — he says, "Get rid of them."

"But they must have paid thousands for this stuff."

"Don't worry about it. The worst thing you can do is publish something that doesn't represent your idea of what this magazine should be."

Something else was bothersome. There was a certain fuzziness around the edges of the letters with which articles were commissioned. The terms were never quite spelled out.

"What you should do," B. said, "is state the kill fee very clearly. Since you people pay miserably, make it half."

His were the only two lessons I ever got in managing editorship, and all I really needed, because the world was shoving subjects in my face.

Mademoiselle's readers bought it because it was a fashion magazine. Anything else, the fiction as well, was lagniappe. Since we didn't have to use the features to sell an issue — if we had, we couldn't have run much beyond articles on sex and diets, because only they made surefire cover lines — we could commission whatever interested *us*. What interested us was eventually codified as "popular culture," "the counterculture," and "feminism." But we never used those terms; we never even knew them. Instead we said, "I heard about this commune in the Berkshires that's led by a kid who's the reincarnation of Saint Peter, so I thought I might go up there for a weekend. . . ." or "How about we use rock stars on the fashion pages? Grace Slick is pretty, so we could use her for a beauty shot, and if Aretha Franklin wants to model something, we could always stick her behind a tree." Which we did.

We ran articles on what we called the Women's Movement, and when *Ms.* was born, we yawned and compared it to *Popular Science* at the same time that we were angry because of all the press it got. Why wasn't anybody looking at us? Why hadn't anyone noticed that we ran articles with titles like "No More Ms. Nice Girl" and writers like Rebecca West, not to mention a passel of very young writers on rock, most of whom could not write well but who for a brief time had cornered the market because nobody else knew anything about the subject? We grouched, we complained, and eventually we relaxed. We were true amateurs, and what we did, we did for love.

Here is Roger, come to my office with his morning coffee, brewed by a black woman named Cora, whose job it is to stand in the hallway behind the coffee urn from nine to ten and greet us white warriors. Roger has transferred his coffee into his big pewter cup and is settling down for our daily chat.

Between us, Roger and I have seen almost every bad movie made between 1935 and maybe 1960, and they form the substructure of our every conversation, especially when we are in the art department. "Don't you find her just a teeny bit reminiscent of the unforgettable Vera Hruba Ralston?" I say, peering through the magnifying glass at the Ektachromes spread on the light table. He looks through his glass at the blond model. "I don't know," he answers. "I would have said Marie Windsor." Were we not to see each other again for thirty years, his first words on meeting me would be something like "Seen any good Faith Domergue movies lately?"

Later today he and I and B.T.B. will be looking at the cover tries. B.T.B.'s response is predictable. "She's got a mutt face," she'll say of the pug-nosed and strong-chinned. Our response is predictable, too. If the sitter is a crop-haired girl much beloved by the fashion department but not by us, we will once more point out her resemblance to Flora Robson. "God, you people are cruel," one of the editors in the college and career department always says when she hears us talking. But we are not cruel. It's just that people whose business is fashion look at models with the same eyes with which they look at a bust dart ("Godawful") or a Rudi Gernreich ("divine!"). One way or another, everything is merch.

There is a clatter in the corridor. Leo, wearing the shaggy coat (it looks like a bearskin) he bought on sale at Saks, has arrived, scattering bon mots as he goes. "Tell all," he commands as Roger and I walk in his door.

I spend a lot of time with Leo. His career, and indeed his identity, depend on keeping up with what's going on. Nobody's going to catch Leo napping! No sir! Mention a new group, a new book, or a new art gallery and Leo's heard it/read it/seen it first.

It is to keep up that Leo climbed endless steps to the balcony of a Lower East Side Loews where Tim Leary, barefoot

in white pajamas, told us to turn on and tune out or something
like that while a girl in a leotard attempted Martha Graham
movements behind a backlighted scrim. Later we went to Rat-
ner's for farina pudding.

"I've seen better high masses," I said airily.

"But that, our Mary, is what this was all about."

He had nothing to say, however, when I dragged him to the
Ike and Tina Turner Revue. Ike talked dirty, Tina humped the
mike, and Leo sat impassive. "I am," he told me once, "a Jewish
puritan. Whereas you, our Mary, are a Catholic prig."

Returned from movies, he gave us capsule reviews. The
cast of *Ship of Fools,* for instance, he described as "everyone
who was not otherwise employed." Staying in London, he sent
us letters to be read aloud. "I can't go into details now but you
must remind me to tell you about Cecil Beaton's party for
Audrey Hepburn where I had a long talk with Princess Margaret. . . ." Yes, we would remind him. We would hang on his
every word.

Tonight Leo is taking me to a screening. What is nice
about a screening, apart from the facts that it is free and that
the seats are as comfortable as club chairs, is the sense it gives
the audience of belonging to a fraternity. I am not at screenings
often enough to recognize anyone, but I can recognize the tie
that binds. The viewers loll in their chairs, they exchange few
words in the elevator going down, but no matter how long they
have done this, no matter how boring the film is, they have
experienced the exquisite pleasure of seeing it first. First! God,
how tired I will get of that word — and that obsession — one
day!

Around noontime I am taking a writer out for lunch at a
restaurant in the East Forties called Cheval Blanc. Cheval Blanc
has the kind of French food that reminds me of the days when
our crowd, B.'s and mine, had innocent mouths, when we
found any pâté, however cold and dry, exciting and always

ordered crème caramel for the joy of giving the proper Yiddish-sounding, soon-to-spit "khr" to "crème." The woman who runs Cheval Blanc is strict about men wearing jackets and keeps a spare for those who do not. Once she forced it on our rock columnist, a very short young man whose fingertips barely emerged from its gorilla-length sleeves. But at least she does not forbid women in pantsuits a table, like some of the restaurateurs farther uptown, although she did frown the day our sex columnist showed up in rayon lounging pajamas. The exterminator had arrived unexpectedly, the columnist announced in her piercing Australian chirp, and she couldn't get to her closet for the bug bombs.

Now, though, there is just enough time to make a few phone calls and dictate a few letters. No, wait. B.T.B. is calling a short meeting in her office. She is not at all happy about our photographing swimsuits in Miami instead of Bermuda. Isn't Miami just a little bit . . . common? The fashion editor explains. It's been raining in Bermuda. Chilly, too. And the magazine's got a due bill at a hotel in Miami, which is a good thing, because we've just about exhausted the travel budget.

There! That's settled. The photographer, a fashion editor, and two models will leave for Miami at the end of the week, along with a stack of swimsuits packed in a long box called the coffin. B.T.B. reaches for her lipstick. So do I. So do the fashion editors: they're on their way to the market. Our perfumes — Diorissimo and Madame Rochas and Femme and my Vent Vert — meet and mingle; the sun hits B.T.B.'s Georgian chandelier; B.T.B. slides a tortured foot out of her Delman pump, then slides it back in again. "Women!" she says fondly. "We *are* a silly sex."

B.T.B. was punctilious about my hours. On the rare evenings I worked late, I could put a cab on petty cash, first having fought with the feral boys who lined up outside the Lexington Avenue entrance of Grand Central, grabbing taxis and demanding ransom in the shape of a tip before they would take their hands off the door handles. But most of the time I could leave the office at rush hour, swept up with half the city toward the subways and the buses.

The lobby of the Graybar Building debouched directly into Grand Central Terminal, so there was no need to go outdoors to get home. Instead I descended a dark, broad staircase near the Lexington Avenue entrance, walked the equivalent of a city block or two, then went down a narrow staircase to the shuttle. My father used to talk about "hopping the shuttle," and now I was hopping it, to career across town to Times Square.

At Times Square, I press my shoulder bag to my side with my right arm, grasp it with my left hand, and, holding my breath against the stink of urine, walk quickly to the IRT–Seventh Avenue line.

Across the way, on the uptown platform, people are packed as densely as sardines, and when a subway arrives they will move in one mindless surge toward its doors. Getting on an uptown train at rush hour is both a game and a shoving match: you can either get into the spirit of the mob or be enraged by the crush and, all too often, the feel of a stiffening penis against your back. To live downtown, however, is to be always going against the traffic, until Thirty-fourth Street, where the Macy's shoppers arrive, lugging their shopping bags and — many of them — composing their souls for the long haul to Brooklyn. They settle their shopping bags along the floor, stare dully at the ads for hemorrhoid cures and cigarettes. The youngest of them bring out paperbacks; the scattering of men lean forward, their elbows on their knees, and study the morning's tabloids.

Fourteenth Street! I rise, skirt the shopping bags and the

occasional extended leg, and leave the car. Straight ahead is the Twelfth Street exit, my exit, and the entrance to another world.

At my left is a big community garden, built on the site of the old Loew's Sheridan, from whose balcony I saw *Rock Around the Clock* and *The Rains of Ranchipur* and *Them!* At my right is the Maritime Trades Building, its porthole windows dark and empty. Ahead is the Greenwich Theater and a thin line of ticket buyers, and beyond it West Twelfth Street, which, in just one short block, has a huge garage, several decaying tenements, and a string of nineteenth-century houses. The only sound is that of my heels on the cement sidewalk.

The traffic is light on Eighth Avenue, and there is none whatsoever on Jane Street. No strollers either. It is a little early for the gang at the No-Name Bar to gather, and the fat man who runs the delicatessen at the corner is looking at an empty store. I lift the latch on the iron gate that leads to the areaway of 44 Jane, unlock the metal grille that is the outer door, relock it, and unlock the wooden inner door. Nobody shouts, "Mommy's home!" Snow White and Rose Red, bathed, fed, and bathrobed, are sitting in the kitchen with Ann, the housekeeper who arrived when Hoppy retired, watching an *I Love Lucy* rerun.

It is not that they are not glad to see me, because they are, and they will be especially glad when, later on tonight, I read them *Eloise* or tell them once again the gripping story of Mary Lee Cantwell, Lost in the Hurricane. But since nine o'clock this morning, they have lived a life to which I have no access. Parents have limited access to their children's lives anyway, but my exclusion is absolute. I am not around.

Rose Red, however, tries very hard to keep me informed. Snow White is old enough to be a charming companion to her father, and on the Saturdays when he is around he takes her out to lunch or to a matinee. *She Loves Me* is her favorite show; she will sing "A Trip to the Library" at the drop of a hint.

Mag, though, is too young for theater. When she and I and her sister went to a revival of *On the Town* (they squealed when they heard "Christopher Street, Christopher Street/Right in the heart of Greenwich Village"), she sat politely on her up-folded seat, the only way she could see over the heads in front of her, kicking her bored legs up and down, up and down. So we spend our Saturday afternoons on long walks, retracing her week.

"This," she says, pausing at a house on West Fourth Street, "is where Ann stopped to tie my shoe." We move along to West Eleventh. "This is where I lost my ball." We enter a variety store for a new one. "They know me here!" she crows.

At Abingdon Square, a dusty triangle with a sandpit, several struggling trees, and some faded benches, I lift her into one of the metal swings and pull down the safety bar. "Have you ever seen the squirrels that live here?" she asks. No, I have not.

When their school reports from St. Luke's arrive, I read about the red skirt that Katie likes to put on during dress-up hour and that she tells her teacher is beautiful. She likes to cook at the play stove in the kitchen corner, too, and pretend to put on makeup from the bag of make-believe cosmetics I gave her for her birthday. Mag, I read, sleeps very soundly at nap-time. But I have never been there when Katie rushed home from school to talk about what she cooked on the cardboard stove, nor have I ever seen Margaret flushed and sleepy after an hour on her little cot. I do not even know which blanket she took from home to cram in her cubby. I am stuffed with memories, so many memories that today they spill over into my dreams and strike me — right across the face — when I am not expecting them. But I do not have these.

I doubt that those two little girls who are watching Lucy

and Ethel fill their faces with chocolates, who are soon to be tucked into what I — and my mother, and indeed all mothers — call "your own little bed," have spent a day that was darkened by my absence. Although we will never know this for certain, the day may even have been the brighter for it. But tonight, when they drift off to sleep and into a place where no one can follow them, they will take with them bits and pieces of lives in which, almost from the beginning, I, their mother, have played no part.

· 4 ·

THERE WAS QUIET, and there was no sex. And a marriage without sex, I realized at last, is a desert.

I had always liked sleeping alone in monkish little beds. Their narrowness helped exclude everyone who had brushed up against me during the day. Once B. had objected to my dark and silent steals, pillow under arm, clock in hand, to the small bed in the small room next to the children. He did not object any longer. When I did sleep in our bed, no hand came out and touched my belly. I asked if there was another woman. Yes, yes, those very words; there are no new ones. He said no.

In February, B. went to Guadalupe for "a rest," and to "lie in the sun." There was, as he knew, no question of my going. I have my father's pale Irish skin, and a beach is a skillet to me.

The day he was due back, a storm came and shut down the airports, and I, not knowing whether he had left the island, called his hotel. The desk clerk spoke an incomprehensible patois, so I called B.'s office and asked for his secretary, a plump young girl who often babysat for us and about whose weight he fretted. Certain that the problem was glandular, he had even sent her to our doctor. When I, who had written reams of copy about diets, said idly that almost all excess weight was due to overeating, he barked, "You don't know what you're talking about," then closed his mouth in a thin, mean line.

His secretary, I was told, was in Florida.

I did not know who was where, did not know for sure for years, and in any case it does not matter now. But I can still feel the cold that iced me, the cold that Emily Dickinson called "zero at the bone."

I can still feel the cold on Hudson Street, too, and the way the wind was whipping up off the river, and the tunnels of snow through which I walked all the way down to St. Luke's Place, trying to exercise away something my body knew long before the message reached my brain.

When, a few hours later, the key turned in the lock of the front door, I jumped up from the kitchen table, where Kate and Mag and I were having supper, ran into the hall, and hugged him. His eyes were opaque. Years before he had gone to Jamaica with friends, and sung "Take me to Jamaica where de rum come from" for the children and me, and done a little dance, and spoken hilariously, happily, of lizards and beaches and mysterious insects. I asked about Guadalupe. "You wouldn't have liked it," he said.

"Maybe if you behaved like Irene Dunne in *The Awful Truth*," Leo suggested. "You know. Lively laughter and all that."

I tried lively laughter. I sat in the living room chattering. B. sucked on his pipe. But sometimes he, too, tried lively laughter. "There are all kinds of people you could marry if you got rid of me," he said.

"Name one."

He named a few bachelors. We laughed immoderately. Such fun!

*   *   *

In June the guest editors arrived at *Mademoiselle,* eager to work on the August issue, which in truth was already close to complete, and after a few weeks of hanging around the office, even more eager to speak of being "exploited." Part of their month in New York now involved a week in a foreign country. For years I had hankered for a free trip with what we called the g.e.'s. Israel was not what I had in mind.

I hated Tel Aviv, of which I recall little but stucco apartment houses built on stilts, with balconies closed by corrugated aluminum doors. The women's army camp we toured was similar to the Girl Scout camp I had gone to when I was twelve, and struck me as about as serious. Israeli men, I decided, would kill rather than queue, and the food left me seven pounds lighter. But everything — the heat, the dryness, the militarism, the chauvinism that had a guide claiming that even the stars were brighter over Israel — receded in the face of my realization that I was in the Holy Land.

I became a pilgrim, returned to Sunday school, returned to stations of the cross and purple-wrapped crucifixes on Good Friday and quick childish prayers to Jesus to "please help me be a good person." We stayed in a kibbutz on the Sea of Galilee, and one evening before dinner I went out to the dock, took off my sneakers, and stuck my feet in the water for a kind of inverted baptism.

For three days I walked through the old quarter of Jerusalem, which is sixteenth century, Turkish, built on ruins, and probably unmappable, through sudden spills of light and fly-covered fruit and taunting, stone-throwing Arab children and rug sellers and Arab men with blue eyes (Crusader remnants, I told myself) who wore gilt-edged burnooses over their striped robes and kept their hands cupped over their crotches.

Walking along the Via Dolorosa, I touched my fingers to its walls, and when a man excavating a trench near the Temple of Solomon tossed up a pot handle he had just uncovered, I wrapped it in my underpants and hid it in my suitcase for the journey home.

A guest editor and I went to the Wailing Wall and, shy and scared, stood well back from the chanting women. Finally I said, "Let's go to the wall. It's ours, too," and we moved forward to face the stones. Tearing a page from my pocket diary, I scribbled a prayer that our family be kept together, and watching to see how the murmurous, davening women did it, I shoved it in a crack.

That night I wandered into a park near the hotel and could find no exit. It was very dark and the trees had no foliage, only white bones of branches. Panicking, I ran along what seemed miles of wire fence until a gate loomed and freed me.

I bought small wooden camels for the children and a Bedouin's embroidered caftan for myself and a blue-and-white-striped robe like those I had seen on the Arab men for B. He smiled awkwardly and, even before he tried it on, said it did not fit. But it did fit, I knew. It would fit anyone short of a dwarf. So I gave it to Leo, who said he would wear it for his at-homes. And I pinned my future on the paper stuck in the Wailing Wall.

A month later. A Saturday afternoon in a little house, no more than one room, really, in Provincetown. The children are in Rhode Island with my mother for a month and I am spending the weekend with a friend from the office. I have just put down the telephone. My sister is expecting a baby at any minute, so I keep checking on her. Using my impending aunthood as an excuse, I keep checking on my husband, too. I need to hear his voice, to know that he is still at 44 Jane Street and that life is proceeding as usual.

My hostess is weeping. She has been twice married, but she has no children. Doesn't like them. Doesn't want them. She has, though, been a mother to men, over and over again.

The first of her men that I remember was very young, with red hair and a shiftiness so apparent one could sniff it. Properly nurtured, she claimed, he would turn into the most adventurous of entrepreneurs, which he did. In a sense. He lifted her credit cards.

The second, who was very handsome, had had a rotten childhood, for which she, in return for companionship (and sex), was prepared to compensate. That rotten childhood, however, had left him with a child's instinct for the jugular, and the more she built him up, the more he tore her down.

My friend is weeping because her boyfriend, a homosexual she was determined to straighten out, has left her for a man. "Why?" she is asking me. "Wasn't I enough?"

The next evening, near midnight. A bedroom in a house in Greenwich Village. The phone rings, waking me, who has returned from Provincetown a few hours earlier. It is my brother-in-law, announcing the birth of my first and only niece. I go to the kitchen, pour a cognac, and toast her alone. My children are, of course, in Bristol. And my husband? I do not know. The front door of 44 Jane Street opened on an empty house. Even so, I, like my friend with the little house on Cape Cod, still believe that there is nothing in a man that a hug and a kiss cannot heal.

With the children away I hoped we could talk, but what about? The few times I mentioned his secretary, he made me feel ashamed of my tortuous, tentative sentences.

"But why did she stay at the house while I was in Israel?" I asked. (A friend of his had told me.)

"I needed help with the children," he said, and shut me up.

I tried sex, hoping that my body, which he had loved so much, could serve as a bridge. He always responded, or rather, his penis did, but his disgust with his ever-ready self made ours a sickbed.

It was hot that August, so hot the kitchen was unbearable, so I would suggest little dinners in Little Italy. Out into the steamy streets we would go and hail a cab to downtown and the perilous flight of steps that led to the Grotta Azzurra. The stuffed artichokes and spaghetti were no better at the Grotta Azzurra than at anyplace else in Little Italy, but during the years when, like babies, we were testing the world with our tongues, the restaurant seemed to us the most "authentic," the most evocative of a southern Italy about which, in truth, we knew nothing whatsoever.

The Grotta Azzurra was invariably noisy, but the only sound I recall is that of my voice, reasonable, charming, skating over hysteria, ashamed to plead when he spoke of moving out. In bed after one of those dinners, I said, "But I could never forget the way your skin smells."

"I have ambivalent feelings about you, too."

That was not what I meant at all.

At Dr. Franklin's I cried until I retched, stuttering about how I had brought my whole life tumbling about me, just like my mother had said I would.

"You should get out of the house," Dr. Franklin said. "You should go to a hospital for a few days and rest."

"No, I can't," I said, nose streaming. "He'll say you put me in a hospital because I'm insane, and he'll take the children away from me."

Dr. Franklin thought I was being paranoid, but time proved me right. A long time later, when words like "separation agreement" and "alimony" and "Mexican judge" flew, batlike, through our home, "custody" was accompanied by a threat to question my sanity in court — "unless you sign." Unless you sign, unless you sign, unless you sign. So many heads, accused of so many crimes, have bowed to "unless you sign."

In the end there was a September night when I sat, legs crossed under me, in the big blue wing chair in the dining room and cried until it seemed my intestines would spill from my mouth, afraid to put my bare feet to the floor, afraid the chill would be irreversible. My husband stayed upstairs. He would not leave until I gave him permission.

How can you hear this? I could never stand to let you cry like this, I thought, and huddled in the wing chair until morning.

When I went upstairs, B. said, "You're killing me," and I, finally guilty of the murder I was always afraid I would commit, said, "Then I guess you'd better leave."

It is always a soap opera. The backgrounds, because I was peripatetic, were more exotic than most, but the dialogue and the situations were the usual. No matter who you are or what has gone into your life, the end of a marriage becomes, when meted out in words, the same old story.

Once in a while one surfaces to courage, one makes a stand. But most of the time one is talking and living the banal. You listen for footsteps coming down the street, but you don't hear the ones you recognize. You wait for the key to turn in the lock, and it does not. The bed seems a prairie and the sheets still smell of him, and in the supermarket you stick your hand in the meat bin for a roast and withdraw it when you realize that a chop is enough. Your married friends avert their eyes if they run into you and do not invite you for dinner, because they figure losing is contagious. Besides, you might cry. You will not, but never mind. It is always the same.

I did not believe in divorce, at least not for people with two young children. I believed in marriage counselors and psychiatrists and will and, above all, responsibility. When B. telephoned and said, "I want a new life and a new wife," I was incredulous.

Blind to his transgressions, I proceeded, with the logic I

used to block hysteria, to define my own. The definition was rigidly, exasperatingly Catholic. "There is a difference," I said to Dr. Franklin, "between sins of omission and sins of commission. The first are negative acts, the second positive. You see, it's not what I *did* do, it's what I *didn't* do, so I am guilty of the first."

"Get *mad*, Mary, get *mad*," friends said when I reported on midnight phone calls from my husband — exhortations to see a lawyer, pleas — no, orders — to release him to the bliss promised by a life with his secretary. "I can't," I would whimper. "I drove him to this. It's my fault. I . . . ," and then I'd stop, unwilling to speak of the nights I got into bed and turned my back, of the day in Bristol many years before when, faced with my mother's unspoken but unyielding opposition to my marrying a Jew, he stood in my old playroom and cried, "What's wrong with me, Mary Lee? What's *wrong?*"

I remembered too much: his tears when he saw me in the pale blue nightgown a friend had given me for our wedding night; the day when I was in a cab stopped at a traffic light and he, coincidentally crossing on the same light, walked up to the cab and slid a book he had just bought me through the half-open window; the boy in the Puerto Rican revolutionary suit carrying peanut-butter sandwiches to Central Park.

"He's behaving like a monster," the same friends said.

"If he is, it's because I made him one," I said, knowing myself for a sinner. The only kind of absolution I understood or could accept now came with the *clap!* of the confessional window.

There is a church on West Fourteenth Street, Irish-immigrant Gothic, with a parochial school, Saturday night bingo, and electric vigil lights that snap on when you put a dime in the slot. I went there one October night when the children were away.

It was raining very hard and I was wearing a trenchcoat and a scarf, conscious of the fact that being tear-stained and black Irish, I probably looked like an IRA widow. It is that self-consciousness, not courage or religious convictions, that keeps people like me alive. How can we watch our own high dramas if we are not around to see them? We are always two people, the star and the spectator, and it is the latter that keeps the former working.

It was the usual rectory office — cheap lace curtains, a desk, old plush chairs, the smell of disinfectant and floor wax — and he seemed the usual priest — in his forties, plump, one leg struggling to cross the other at the thigh. But he was not the usual priest. He was a psychology professor on leave from a midwestern university to do fieldwork among the urban poor.

He did not scold me for my apostasy or for the civil ceremony that was my wedding or for my not sending Katherine and Margaret to Sunday school. He said instead that he regretted what the Catholic Church, his Church, had done to me. When I said that I wanted to die, he did not tell me that I had to live for the children's sake. He said, "Jesus would be kinder to you than you are to yourself." When I told him I thought myself an adulterer because I had lusted for Philippe, he said, "You are confusing the wish for the deed. Did we teach you to do that? If so, I am sorry." He was a nice man, but he did not give me four Our Fathers, three Hail Marys, and some rules to live by, so I left with my sins intact.

Somewhere in this world there was an Irish priest with a face like Samuel Beckett's and a mind like St. Paul's. He was laying down the law, confirming the verities, and scaring his parishioners. That was the kind of priest I had known as a child and the kind I looked for and did not find on Fourteenth Street. Raised in a church that manufactured crutches for its communicants, I had thrown mine away. Now I needed them again. But during the years that I was out courting damnation, the church, it appeared, had gone out of the business.

A few months later I went to Europe to work with a photographer for three weeks. For years I had kept travel diaries — notes on where we had been and what we had eaten and what things had cost — and now they were filling up with prayers and pleas and fragmented memories of dreams. "Dreamed I was walking through the Sahara. . . . Dreamed I saw B. kissing a tall, thin, pretty girl. . . . Dreamed about Papa. He was wearing a brown suit and a felt hat." During the day I interviewed fashionable young women about their lives in London and Paris, and at night I would scribble in the diaries, crying, then turn to the detective stories that since childhood had lulled me to sleep. "To bed with Michael Innes," I would write. "To bed with Nicholas Blake."

After twelve days, the photographer and I went to Amsterdam. I hate Amsterdam. I hate cold ham and cheese at breakfast and the car-clogged streets and the damp that rises from the canals, and I have memories of the ladies' room in the Rijksmuseum that put the lie to the legend of old Dutch cleansers. I had been in Amsterdam once before. This time and then, the rain was constant.

One evening when it was dark but too early for dinner and my room was getting colder and grayer and quieter and I had nothing more to add to those half-hysterical travel notes, I felt I had to move or die.

I called New York and spoke to Ann, who said my husband had taken the children out for supper and told her that he would never live at home again. The kind of woman who would be in the front row at a hanging, she bustled about, a self-appointed emissary between my husband and myself, dispensing poison. She bore me no malice, but her allegiance was to the male heads of households, and she loved theater. "I knew something was up, Mrs. L. . . . You're too innocent, Mrs. L. . . . You'd better hurry up and marry again, Mrs. L., 'cause once those children grow, ain't no man comes to this house gonna look at you."

Then I spoke to the children. Kate said she missed me, and Margaret, who was reading *Winnie-the-Pooh,* said nothing but "Tiddly pom pom pom, tiddly pom pom pom." I sat on the edge of the bed, crying as always, wanting to die, wishing the decision would be taken from me, and, also as always, mocking myself. *How like you, Mary Lee,* I thought, *to have made sure you were cracking up in Amsterdam rather than in Westport, Connecticut.*

Oh yes, move or die. When in doubt, walk. I went to the hotel lobby, asked for the nearest Catholic church, and went outside to cross an enormous cobblestone square. The church was several hundred yards up a neon-lit street.

Once I would have been able to fantasize myself into a romantic figure moving, lonely and mysterious, through a foreign city. This time the magic didn't work. I was just a woman in her thirties whose husband didn't want her, looking for a priest who would take her out of the pain and put her back in a world where a good act of contrition equaled morphine.

A man and a woman were praying at the back of the church (married! kneeling together!), and when they rose to leave, I asked how I could find the priest. I was crying again, obviously not a person one would want to be around, so they pointed to a bellpull and fled.

The sexton was old and lame, and when he saw the tears asked if I wanted to make a confession. No, I mumbled, I just want to see a priest. When he limped back a few minutes later and said, "The father will see you now," I felt a weight sliding off my body, a kind of thumb-sucking, milk-glutted peace.

The father. To me, as I followed the sexton to a door near the altar, the word meant God, the priest, and, above all, Papa.

The father was a small blond man in a pale gray flannel suit and a necktie. He lit a gas fire, then sat silent while I spoke incoherently of the husband to whom I had been a bad wife and the children to whom I did not believe I could be a good mother. I told him that I had been married by a judge and that I had not taken Communion since I was twenty-one, and that I would like to come back to the Church but that if I thought there was the slightest chance my husband would come home, I knew I would reject Catholicism all over again.

His English was thickly accented and hesitant, and he stared at me all the time he spoke — his eyebrows and lashes were, I remember, white — trying to make his eyes help his clumsy tongue. He said he would pray that I would have the strength I needed for my children. He said strength was what I should pray for as well. He said I must be more merciful to myself. And he said that I was honest, and that he would rather have me honest and outside the Church than dishonest and within it. I left, both frightened that I could not find my way back to the nest and giddy because a priest, a *priest,* had given me permission to fly. It was an absolution, of sorts.

· 5 ·

Two and three and even four times a week (it took two years to pay the bill), I emerged from the IRT at Seventy-second Street to walk to West End Avenue and Dr. Franklin. The elderly people who had sat on the benches on the scruffy grass median that ran along Broadway were companioned now by junkies; the pastry shops that had sold strudel and hamentaschen and those little butter cookies that, judging by the bakeries, Jewish families eat by the thousands were starting to disappear; the lights were off behind the big window in the shop of the tailor who had made my green tweed suit. Seventy-second Street was going down, down, down, and living on the Upper West Side had begun to take a certain bravado.

My dreams, I told Dr. Franklin, were awful. In them my husband and father were so confused that I did not know which was which, or who had died, or what was dead. Describing them, I became even more confused. I said "When I died" when I meant "When my father died." I would start to say "B." and it came out "Papa." I babbled, but I never really talked — except, maybe, about others. By now everyone I knew had a psychiatrist — always called a headshrinker — and where once what was said between the two of you was as sacred as confession, it had now become the stuff of lunch-hour conversations. But not my conversations. Even if I had wanted to, I would not have known what to say. Because I never really said anything, besides those curious slips of the tongue, to Dr. Franklin.

Introspection, I figured, was a luxury reserved for those who could afford a peek into the subconscious. I could not. Better I should allow myself the pleasure of opacity and, with Dr. Franklin's help, scuttle along as best I could. Otherwise, like a child taking a watch apart to see how it works, I might stop the tick.

Dr. Franklin had become impatient — I think — and he had changed, presumably with the times. Where once he had sat silent, his notebook in his lap, he was now vocal, even physical. When I cried so hard I bent my head to my knees and wet my skirt with tears and the run from my nose, he put his arm around my shoulders and raised me back into the world. When I tried to run from his office, enraged because he said that now I seemed a woman, and a sexy one at that, compared to the sexless child he had once treated, he wrestled me back to the chair, locked the door, and said, "You're going to sit there and tell me why being called a sexy woman terrifies you."

I did not tell him, because I pretended I did not know. But I did have half the answer. Being told I was sexy made me sick to my stomach, partly because it was my psychiatrist who said so and mostly because it was anathema to someone who was, however lapsed, a true child of a church that was far more Irish than it was Roman. But a woman? What was that? My secondary sex characteristics were not such as to drive the point home, and the brain, I had assumed, was androgynous. The discrimination practiced by New England Protestants in the name of God and by New York Jews in the name of Spain had kept me aware that I was a Catholic. But an education at a women's college and jobs on a women's magazine had kept me innocent of sexism. My father's daughter, oblivious of my mother, I inhabited an indeterminate sexual territory, not wholly female, certainly not male, unconsciously neuter. If anyone had ever asked me what I was, I might have replied, "A Mary."

Some women at the office were joining consciousness-raising groups. When they suggested my coming along, I drew back, afraid to have anyone but Dr. Franklin picking at my head. I was interested in feminism as a subject to be explored and exploited for magazine articles, but faced with a crusade, I was, as ever, detached. The only authorities I had accepted were God the father and God the husband, and I felt a chill — still do — whenever I heard someone preaching. So if I embraced feminism, I did so in the name of economics and editorial intelligence and not for the sake of illumining the inner life.

One day a minor movement star came to the office. Pretty, articulate, impassioned, she was a thorough fraud. On being introduced, she snubbed me until she found out who my husband was, then cozied up like a cat looking for a scratching. Thanks to a man whom she knew to be successful, I had acquired an identity — his — and was thus a desirable acquaintance.

She was forming a new consciousness-raising group that night, and asked if I would like to sit in at the birth.

There were about twenty women in her apartment, but I recall only three. A belly dancer who said that she used men sexually as casually as men used women, and that it was a sensible arrangement, on the whole. A recent medical school dropout, dropped out because she could not stand the jibes and pressures from her male teachers and fellow students. A young, well-dressed mother who was eager to join a group in New York because the summer she had been part of one on Long Island had been the happiest of her life. "We petitioned the mayor to let us parade on Equality Day and we won. It was the first time I'd ever really defied a man, and I was so proud."

I could not identify with any of the women. In fact they puzzled me. I did not believe that the belly dancer was as casual about sex as she claimed. It was unlikely that any male could have driven me out of school, and the only men I was conscious of having had power over me were my father and my husband, neither of whom I lumped with men. A few months later, however, when I wanted to tape a group for an article, I called one of the women. Would the group allow it? And would they discuss their sexuality?

I do not know why they permitted the intrusion. Perhaps it was my unexpected eloquence when, at a prior confrontation (we used that word a lot then), I said, "I've never known the left or the right not to grab a soapbox when it was offered to them. So here you are — you call yourselves the mainstream of feminism — turning one down. No wonder the people in the middle aren't heard. You don't know how to use the media." "Media" was another word we used a lot. So, for that matter, was "used."

We met in an apartment on East Ninety-sixth Street, which is the great divide. Cross it and you're in Harlem. The group, shrunk to eight women, was so uniformly white, middle-class, clean, and well syllabled that we looked like a Junior League steering committee. I could not imagine any dialogue coming out of this evening that could not be reported in an alumnae magazine.

The first speaker, the woman I had met at the office, had separated from her husband a few months previously. In the interim she had gone to bed with her husband's closest friend ("He kept making noises — *unh, unh, unh* — and it was wonderful") and nine other men. Only one experience had been unsatisfactory: "He came like within a minute or two, like immediately." Temporarily between men, she had mastered masturbation. "Now I feel autonomous, my own woman. Besides, any way you get it, it's nice."

Another woman, blond, pink-cheeked, a monument to Peck & Peck, was a teacher at the city's fanciest girls' school. She had been taught to masturbate when very young by her boyfriend and could not attain orgasm any other way, although she had tried every other way with all kinds of men, one of whom said she reminded him of his daughter. "I think he was using me," she said.

A third, the ex-wife of an editor I knew slightly, had spent her childhood in closets and under bushes with a flashlight, checking out male and female genitalia; her adolescence in bed with other girls; and her maturity in bed with men other than her husband. The last, she told us, was "purely satisfying."

The fourth . . . no matter. For years I kept the transcript in a file, and now it is hidden, assuming it still exists at all, in a place always referred to as "Forty-fifth Street." Forty-fifth Street is where Condé Nast sent old manuscripts and letters to die. This manuscript, however, should be in a time capsule. Words jump out of it, I remember — "orgasm," "autonomous," "beautiful, that's really beautiful" — that mark its year, 1970, as surely as a date stamp.

Now I would not be surprised by what was said that night, but I was then, because I discovered that I did not know much about women. That nobody knew much about women. I began to think about myself as a woman. What is one, besides the obvious? Or is the obvious what one is? Where did I fit in? *Did* I fit in? If feminism did nothing else, it gave me a sex, my own. Whether that is one step forward or one step back depends, of course, on how you look at it.

Because I found working easier than living (I was still making a distinction between the two), I assigned myself and a close friend, Amy Gross, to an article about Stephen, a former se- manticist who, guru to hundreds, had piled his disciples into schoolbuses and led a caravan across the United States, preach- ing the gospel according to himself. His lesson was that "we are all monkeys living on the same rock" and that we have to keep the rock clean or die in the garbage. I could not fault the message, but Stephen's disciples were dismaying. They sat numbly, dumbly during his discourses, they followed him as donkeys would a carrot, they had given themselves up to his Word. They were kind, sweet people, and talking to them was like eating air.

All the long train ride to Providence, where Stephen was speaking, Amy and I played the sixties games. We compared our horoscopes to our photographer's: the conjunction prom- ised perfection. We tossed the I Ching: the goat was, as usual, in the brambles. And, graduates of the same college, we tried to dig up what little we remembered about Jung and the collec- tive unconscious. When Stephen made his entrance into Brown University's Sayles Hall — so skinny that he looked pumiced, and soaring on peyote — and took off his boots, lotused him- self onto the floor, and sounded his ram's horn, my "Om" was as sonorous as any in that perfect Episcopal room.

The next day I was sitting cross-legged on one of the mattresses that carpeted Stephen's bus, tape recorder between my thighs, dodging the ritual joint, nervously eyeing the dope box, praying the state police wouldn't come over the hill and cart me to jail ("Editor held on drug rap," the headline would read. "Estranged husband sues for child custody"), and listening to Stephen talk about tantric yoga, satanism, Freud, Hindu chakras, acid, energy, and craziness.

"What's insanity?" I asked.

Insanity, it seemed, was optional. "I've been crazy every way imaginable, and I found insanity's just like ticktacktoe. After you've been through it enough times, you know who starts, who finishes, and where it all goes — and it's no longer insanity. It's more of your head. There's a choice about going crazy. You decide it. It's not something that just happens."

Remembering the bed rails, the nurse telling me to pray, that splat when my baby's body and mine hit the pavement, the horror ten years back, I told him that he was wrong, that once I had had the choice taken from me, that — and then I stopped, because Amy and the photographer were overhearing something I had not wanted anyone to know. Stephen did not count. More priest than person, he had heard everything. Once again I was trying to confess.

"You're afraid sanity is a little teacup that you carry around like this" — his hands cupped — "but sanity is really tough. The secret about the mind is, you can't blow it. I can't cop to insanity, and I can't cop to anything that human beings can't handle. There's no refuge outside yourself."

But there was. There was Stephen, at least for the disciples who sat in a circle with us, sipping peppermint-alfalfa tea, sticking wood in the little stove, silent as Trappists. I looked around the bus and imagined giving up the books, the furniture, the job, and moving the children and myself into narrow wooden bunks, leaning on Stephen's perceptions so I would not have to grapple with shaping my own. Stephen was better than opium. I wish I could say it was self-reliance that finally made me turn my head. It was not. It was a sudden desperate wish to be out of that pond and back in the maelstrom, back in the place where there were lots of people like me.

We are in that place, Amy and I, sitting at my dining room table, the pages of the transcript scattered about us, cursing the vagaries of the typing service and chortling as we listen to the tapes with their undersounds of kindling being halved and teacups rattling. Throughout them my voice is a brisk, clear soprano, rather snotty; Amy's is slow, sonorous, sexy. "You *see* what marijuana does to you," I am shouting. "You *see!*" Amy laughs. We bend our heads to our lined yellow pads, congratulating each other when we hit a phrase we think especially apposite.

Without work, who or what will tangle your head, your hands? Everybody needs a tangle. Especially when she can no longer depend on a sideways glance and a cute little laugh to act as a grappling hook.

Women without tangles. Once, on the Costa del Sol, I met three of them. The first had a son in Hong Kong, a daughter in Manhattan, a small condominium on the beach, and a little alimony. She went on quickie package tours ("Badly arranged, my dear, I can't tell you how badly arranged") of Tangiers and Gibraltar and points south, never missed a maid's wedding or a baby's baptism (in a flowered hat and a garden-party dress), and started with gin before noon. She called it "Mr. Juniper."

There was a plump blonde in her fifties who hung out in the midnight bars, the young Spanish fishermen clustered about her like flies about fruit. There had been an evening when she had changed her mind, I was told, and the man who had taken her home bit her naked breast. From then on I never looked at the woman's face. My eyes were fixed on her caftan's deep V, hunting for the scar.

A third, another blonde, had the older woman's little pot-belly, that false pregnancy that blossoms after menopause. Her long thighs shook when she walked, and no amount of swimming, jogging, compulsive housework, and compulsive dieting could bring her back to what she had been. She was not one for Spanish fishermen. She inquired after widowers.

Women without men, women without work. There but for the grace of good typing go I. "But you'll never be like that, Mary," the people whom I was with protested when I confided my fear of ending up on a Spanish barstool with teethmarks on one breast. "I am, I am," I insisted, laughing. They thought I was kidding. I was not.

But I am jumping. Spain and ten days on the Costa del Sol came later. Now I am at 44 Jane Street, bent over a table and a transcript, afraid to look up, because if I do I will see a house with no husband in it and two confused children, one of whom clings to me, the other of whom is slowly, too slowly for me to catch the motion, drifting out to sea.

The saddest thing about sorrow is that it is as evanescent as everything else. One day it dies, leaving a hole as empty as the socket left by an extracted tooth. You keep searching the socket with your tongue, hoping to lick a nerve, hoping for the old shock. But you feel nothing.

A night in a church in Amsterdam, an afternoon in a guru's bus, rise up and take line and color like the visions conjured by acid, but for the rest it is one long night. I snatch at rags. Myself sobbing, pleading with two women who had stolen the cab I had been hailing for blocks because I was late for Dr. Franklin and to miss him was to die. They stared and slammed the door, and the driver rolled up his window before they drove away. Dreaming the old dream about Papa met in a Manhattan crowd. Hearing the telephone ring after midnight, when the children were asleep and I was dozing into the darkness: he demanding a divorce, I alternately begging for another chance and scourging his secretary. But they are rags, and they touch as lightly as rags now. Once snatched, they can be brushed away. They leave behind only a few fibers, little filaments of pain that twinge when I have forgotten to anesthetize myself with talk or work.

A long night, a few rags, a few scenes, and, finally, a day when my head, my body, and — can I say my soul? — were once more in the same place.

It was January, and my mother had been calling all week with reports of Peggy, relayed by Peggy's sister Julia. Peggy was sixty-four, an art teacher in the public schools whom I had known since my childhood. She loved painting and reading and talking and Ireland and Portugal, and ran through life highlighting everyone she knew, like an artist touching up a sitter's hair and skin. Because of Peggy, all of us became a little more beautiful, a little more romantic, a little more interesting, to ourselves as well as to others. To know her was to be presented with infinite possibilities. That was her gift to her friends.

"Julia says Peggy is very tired. She sleeps a lot" . . . "Julia was at the hospital today. She said Peggy's getting very quiet" . . . "Peggy asked Julia to brush her hair, but it hurt her scalp too much and Julia had to stop" . . . "Peggy died last night."

The evening before I went home for the funeral, B. called. Had I seen the lawyer, had I agreed . . . ? My eyes on the clothes I was packing and wet, for once, with grief for someone else, I snapped, "I'm not interested in our divorce or your marriage. Peggy is dead and I'm going home and that's all I care about." As I talked, I realized that Peggy was indeed all I cared about just then, that the death of my friend was more important than the death of my marriage. Of course, if I were married to a friend . . . but I was not, not anymore.

As we walked up the aisle after the service the next morning, my oldest friend whispered, "Whenever I come to a funeral here, I think of your father's and how beautiful it was. Do you remember?" "Yes," I said, and we went to the cemetery and stood by Peggy's grave, a few hundred yards from Papa's.

It was a day like every January day in Bristol: no snow, bare black branches spearing the gray sky, matted brown grass underfoot. In this cemetery my married name was irrelevant, probably unknown or forgotten. I was the Cantwell girl, to some old-timers Mary Lonergan's girl, Margaret Guinan's grandchild. It is possible that someone there was old enough to know that I was Bridget McCarty's great-grandchild. But for a chipped front tooth, I had no feature that had not belonged to them or to my father. My accent was theirs. I was as shocked by divorce as they would have been, and as little equipped to deal with it. I was all of them, and home again, I had slipped imperceptibly into the spin of their lives.

Several days after the funeral, B. agreed to join me at Dr. Franklin's. They had never seen each other, this man I had known for nineteen years and this man I had known for fifteen. My life was divided between the two, and they had never met.

Again I talked and cried, and then I heard my husband's silence, though he spoke, and watched his eyes, which, though they looked, could not see me. "You don't know what it was like for me," he had said a few months back, during one of his midnight phone calls. "All those years of Dr. Franklin and the migraines and that time after Kate was born." And I, stung and sick with memories, said, "But you don't know what it was like for me." That's all it was, really: neither of us ever knew what it was like for the other.

B. left the doctor's office a few minutes before me. I was not cool enough to share an elevator with him, or for us to part casually in simultaneously hailed cabs. Dr. Franklin put his hand on my arm and said, "It's no use, Mary. Let him go."

So I did.

Afterword

FOR A LONG TIME, I have lived on the street down which I used to walk to the garbage pier to watch the Italians from the South Village grooming their cars. The garbage pier is inaccessible to all but sanitation trucks now, and the old pilings are slumped against the supporting rocks and covered with barnacles and that green slippery stuff of which I have never known the name but which is like aqueous moss. Looking down at them, I might imagine that I am in Bristol. The rocks and the lapping water and the smell of brine are precisely the same. But I do not want to imagine an elsewhere. These, the Hudson River and the towers on the New Jersey shore and the Circle Line boats, are what I want to see.

At my back is the meat market. During the day large men in bloodstained coats and hardhats load beef carcasses into trucks and take lunch breaks on the loading docks. At night the prostitutes — young men mostly, usually black and sometimes in drag — come out. They stand in the shadows cast by the warehouses' old metal awnings or, if it's cold, around the fire somebody has started in a rusted metal drum.

They are visible, but the other habitués of the meat market are not. They have disappeared behind unmarked doors and down flights of stairs into the leather bars that have made this place ground zero. At least, I think most of the bars have re-opened — one sees the occasional notice posted on a streetlight — but they are as transient as the sea gulls that sweep the streets for garbage when the river is frozen. One night you see a cluster of men at a doorway; the next night, maybe not. A certain decorum prevails in the meat market. The men in clusters do not look at me, I do not look at them, and the prostitutes keep custody of their eyes.

The street itself is nicer than it used to be. The refrigeration plant at its foot has been turned into an apartment house, as have some of the derelict warehouses, and the block association has planted pear and cherry trees and put evergreens in great big terra-cotta pots. Even so, the street is almost always empty when I come home at night, and my eyes are searchlights, sweeping it from side to side until I reach the front door. My key is out, I look behind me, I turn the knob. Whew! I have trumped the predators again.

My building is one of those that underwent transformation — transfiguration, really. A livery stable built in 1907, it eventually became a warehouse for a meatpacking company. My piece of it, two thirds of the first floor, was its garage. When first I saw it, oil stains had sunk into the cement floor and iron shutters were closed over its tall windows. But two columns stretched sixteen feet to a ribbed tin ceiling, and the space seemed limitless. Two years after I moved in, real estate prices escalated, and I realized that selling it would mean money enough to buy the little house that I had sought all over Greenwich Village. But while I could have crammed my possessions into small rooms, I could no longer have crammed myself. Besides, I had labored for this place as doggedly as Jacob had labored for Rachel.

The thing is, in New York you are always at someone's mercy. The children and I had to move from 44 Jane because Matty needed our duplex for his mother-in-law, and after seven years' residence we had to move from our next place because the landlord wanted it for himself. But we were glad to leave.

He beat his wife and she drank herself into slurred speech and ankles that swelled and spilled over her shoes, and sickness soaked their walls and trickled all the way down into ours. But then there was a kind of sickness in our rooms, too. One midnight I had to search the basement, terrified lest my flash-light land on a pair of small, sneakered feet limp and useless on the floor. But that is another story, and one that is not mine to tell.

We had no place to go, not for the fifteen months it would take to turn the garage into an apartment. Curiously, this was no hardship, for me, at least. Night after night I wrapped cups and saucers and shell frames and a Staffordshire goat and toys long outgrown in sheets of newspaper. I tagged the furniture and put all the sheets and pillows into bureau drawers, and when the truck came to take everything into storage, I was lighter by a million years. Then we started traveling, Rose Red and I (Snow White had gone away), all over Manhattan.

First came two weeks on the top floor of a narrow house on Jane Street, two doors west of the house to which Mary Rogers — Edgar Allan Poe's Marie Roget — said she was going on the August day in 1841 when she disappeared. That house, which belonged to her aunt, is gone, but the one that remains is almost certainly its twin, as are the five other twelve-footers on the south side of Jane Street.

From there we moved to a house as old as the one on Jane Street and a torrid summer on Eighth Avenue. Here we had all four floors, but the living room was so formal we were afraid to sit down, and the kitchen was visited by winged bugs we called Puerto Rican flying cockroaches. We had never seen them before, we have never seen them again, and one day they vanished as suddenly as they had appeared.

After Eighth Avenue, there was Thirteenth Street between Sixth and Seventh Avenues and a few weeks in a basement apartment. All basement apartments are dark, but the landlord had built a staircase from the parlor floor into the garden, which made this one even darker. I cried here all the time, and Rose Red asked timidly, "Is this menopause, Mom? Is this menopause?" "No," I said, "it's only the dark," and cried some more.

Then we moved into the light: a bedroom, living room, bathroom, and kitchen on a high floor in a high-rise on Hudson Street. I had not lived in a place with a doorman since East Twenty-first Street and had forgotten the silence of apartment-house corridors and the secrecy that attends a long line of closed doors. There was safety in living behind a guarded lobby, but we could hear the toilet flushing in the next-door apartment, and the kitchen was no more than a closet. In New York, unless one is very rich and maybe even then, one is always a Goldilocks, trying rooms on for size and seldom finding a "just right."

By now we had run out of sublets, and there was nothing for it but the Chelsea Hotel.

I had passed the Chelsea, which is on West Twenty-third Street, often over the years and been in it three times. The first time I was at a party given by Virgil Thomson for, he said, "the friends of Alice B. Toklas." His suite was a monument to horse-hair upholstery and stained glass windows, and the guests a monument to intellectually posited frumpiness. I remember a lot of women in late middle age with flyaway hair, crocheted sweaters stretched over breasts that had never known bras, and strings of amber beads.

The second time was for a dinner given by a couple who were between apartments and making the best of it. They had draped crepe paper around the tiny dining area and across the peeling ceiling, and the hostess had managed to produce a roasted chicken and a lopsided cake out of an oven that never went above 350 degrees. Still, there was no jollity, no celebration. There couldn't be, not in a room that promised no exit.

The third time I was interviewing an actress in town for a play. Her suite was presentable — "because the producer coughed up a piano and some pictures" — but on leaving it one walked through scarred corridors to a street where old black men, and a few old white men, held sad travesties of cocktail parties with cheap wine in paper bags and a brave bonhomie.

I had a horror of the Chelsea, yet here we were, with three cats, a dog, a few clothes (I kept the rest in trash bags in a corner of my office), our portable television set, and my hot rollers, lodged directly above the room in which Sid Vicious had murdered his girlfriend, Nancy, a few days before. "Did you hear anything?" the plainclothes man who knocked on our door asked. "We're new here," I answered, and tried to make it clear that we were only passing through.

We were not. The next day I shared the Chelsea's one elevator with Thomson, who didn't seem at all surprised on hearing I had moved in. *Maybe he sees me as the kind of woman who sooner or later ends up in the Chelsea Hotel,* I thought. Then I laughed. Obviously, I *was* the kind of woman who sooner or later ends up in the Chelsea Hotel. For eight months.

It was a cold winter, but the radiators shuddered with heat, and in the fireplace the Dura-Flame logs from the delicatessen shook with flame. The water was always hot, and dinner simmered on the stove and scented the room. Rose Red had her schoolbooks, and I books borrowed from friends, and together we watched *Masterpiece Theatre* on the television set. The dog and the three cats nudged us in our sleep, jubilant because they were never more than five feet from their owners, and I felt as if I were pregnant again, not only with Rose Red but with our pets and our few possessions. On the nights that Snow White, slowly returning from sea, stayed over and shared a studio couch with her sister, I would lie awake and listen to their slow, deep breathing. My babies were folded into their mother again, where nothing — short of her death — could harm them.

Then spring came, and with it opened windows that let in the sound of radios and quarrels across the courtyard and the screech of cats. We moved to the Upper East Side, to a friend's apartment so meticulously planned that a cigarette ash blindly dropped would hit an ashtray and light bulbs multiplied like mice. Here there was no sound of flushing from the next-door apartment, the maintenance men moved as swiftly and silently as if they were on wheels, and the doorman's hand was quick to the cab's rear door. But it was not the Village. We could not find any cheap Asian-Cuban restaurants. Everybody dressed to go to the supermarket.

We moved again, a few blocks north, to a bigger apartment, big enough for the man who lived there — with his wife, another of my friends — to spare one room for an office. At eight-thirty, just when I was sitting down to the paper and a second cup of coffee, his staff arrived. There could be no lounging about *en déshabillé*. I was combed, lipsticked, and immaculate by eight.

Finally, the last move, to an apartment in the South Village, in the district of the old printing plants. Rose Red had fled, for two weeks in Connecticut with a classmate who had proper parents and proper beds, and once again I was hanging around, hanging out. One night I walked past an Italian luncheonette that normally closed at seven. A light was burning in the back, so, curious, I peered through the plate glass to see a scene that might have been taking place in Naples: the luncheonette owner's family stripping piles of basil of its leaves for next winter's pesto. The first time I had ever tasted pesto was in Little Italy, only a few blocks away, when B. and I went to the San Gennaro Festival and a band played "I'll Take Manhattan." We danced to it, on a raised platform roped off like a boxing ring. "My God," we kept telling each other, "this is like a movie."

At last the new apartment was ready. The furniture was sprung from storage and we settled back into our own beds. "You must be thrilled," people said. "All that moving around!"

Rose Red was. I was not. There were still so many streets we had not walked, so many stores we had not entered, so many lives we had not tried.

Almost nothing has been discarded, not even the photographs and drawings and mottoes kept on my bulletin board at *Mademoiselle*. I took them with me when I left, all that I retain of that job besides the way my lips, without my willing it, curve into a smile whenever I remember the chatter and the I Ching and "Group order! Group order!" I missed them when I moved on to the *New York Times*. But not much. They had been outgrown.

Where I am now is a very grownup place, and writing editorials is a very grownup occupation. But to me it seems that I have come full circle, that I am copywriting all over again. Describing a dress and describing a social policy take the same set of knacks: the ability to analyze, clarify, and compress. One has to have a point of view, of course, and I am no more skilled in debate now than I was when I tried to tell B. and Jerry about transsubstantiation and Duns Scotus. But once I am seated in front of my computer, everything comes clear. If I have spent a lifetime writing one thing or another, it is because it is the only way I can figure out what I am thinking.

Sometimes I am invited to a publisher's lunch, and then I sit at a long mahogany table staring at the distinguished guest and his (or, occasionally, her) inevitable aides, worrying about forking the baked chicken breast off the platter presented at my left shoulder and wondering if I should put the spoon for my iced tea (the recipe for which is said to have come from the famous Iphigene) on the damask tablecloth or the little plate the glass stands on. The silver is Tiffany's Hampton, the conversation is equally polished, and the guest, seated at the right hand of the publisher and an old pro at forking chicken off platters, exhales success.

When I leave, after the cigars have been passed, the demitasse sipped, and the guest's hand shaken, it is with the momentary illusion that all's well with the world, or could be. Haven't I just been at civilization's epicenter? Haven't I just sipped a perhaps historic iced tea?

Little now can be experienced on its own, not even in Times Square. There is always a point of reference. Walking along Broadway at lunchtime, I am reminded of Allie and me, also at lunchtime, searching for an I. Miller outlet we had heard was in the area. Our college shoes — Bass Weejuns, sneakers, and suede pumps for fraternity parties — were not suitable for the office.

After dark, heading for the subway at Forty-second Street, I try to figure out where Toffenetti's Restaurant was. This corner? That corner? Back there? B. and I never ate at Toffenetti's, but we thrilled to the menu posted in its window, not for its offerings but for the purpleness of its prose. When B. sent a sample to *The New Yorker* (everyone we knew was forever looking for funny bits of prose to send to *The New Yorker*) and it was published, we were as excited as if he had produced a short story.

Strolling down Fifth Avenue after a movie at MoMA, I remember, we would pass the Olivetti typewriter on a stanchion outside the nearby Olivetti showroom. But how nearby? There was a paper in it for passersby, and on it B. would type "the quick brown fox . . ." and I, "My name is Mary and I live on. . . ."

I called Olivetti a few years ago. I wanted to know exactly

where that showroom was. Nobody there knew, or had even heard of it. But that typewriter existed, I'm sure of it, as surely as we did once.

There is no bulletin board in my *Times* office, only Piranesi prints left by my predecessor. My sole addition to the décor is a big color photograph Kate took of Bristol Harbor. But buried under a pile of leaflets on a shelf in back of my desk is a photograph torn from a magazine. It is that famous one of the little Jewish boy who, with his hands up, is being led away to what one supposes was his death. I love that boy in the photograph, because had he lived to adulthood, he would have looked like B. In fact, he *is* B., more surely than the stranger I danced with a few years ago at Margaret's wedding.

At the bottom of the in box on my desk is another photograph — a Xerox, actually, of a photograph — from the May 7, 1961, issue of the Sunday *Times Magazine*. It accompanied an article about Greenwich Village, and is of me and Kate.

I did not know a camera had been aimed at us until I read the article on a Saturday night at 21 Perry Street. I turned to the runover and there it was, a picture of a thin, square-shouldered woman in a Lacoste shirt, white pants, and sneakers pushing a stroller, the kind with a fringed canopy. The child in the stroller is obviously a girl; you can tell by her bonnet.

We have been at Washington Square, I am sure, and now we are going home for supper. Along the way I have been looking, as always, for the little house to which we will move one day, the house that is the material equivalent of Jane Austen's prose. And here it is, in the newspaper of record, a record of one New York woman's stroll with her daughter on a hot spring day in 1961.

I still stroll, all the time, but I doubt I shall ever move again. I will never find a better place. Besides, maybe I do not want to open any more doors. But that is silly. They will open anyway. Still, sometimes I imagine living where Margaret lives:

a pretty little backwater in Brooklyn where every stray cat gets a bowl of Friskies put out for his breakfast and householders sweep their sidewalks every morning. I go there often, for dinner, and breathe deeply of the peace.

The dream lasts only for as long as it takes my cab to cross the Manhattan Bridge, travel west on Chambers Street, and round the corner onto what remains of the West Side Highway. What I see then, at the right, is a line of massive buildings, and what I feel is their power. It is as if I have been given a shot with a kick like a donkey's, a shot of something to which I am terminally addicted.

"Could you wait till I get inside?" I ask the driver. He nods, and stays in place until I unlock the front door of my building. A short flight of steps, and I unlock the door to my apartment. The cats are waiting as I enter; the barely audible pad of their paws is the only sound.

An hour or two with a book, and it is time for sleep. I open the bedroom window, not on a street but on a garden. The noise from traffic, pedestrians, quarrels, late-night drunks cannot penetrate the trees and bushes and these thick brick walls. Even so, I can hear it. The hive. Buzzing.